The Economics of Values, Ideals and Organizations

Values-based organizations are institutions, communities and non-governmental organizations (NGOs) which are inspired by a mission or a vocation – for these groups it is their ideals which are most important to them and economics does not have a way to incorporate that into its analysis. This book provides a short introduction to the economics of values-based organizations.

The book opens with an analysis of some phenomena common to all organizations: the management of vulnerabilities in relationships and the role of incentives, especially in relation to loyalty. Turning to values-based organizations more specifically, the book explores the motivations of their members, how they retain their most motivated people, what happens when the ideals of the organization are perceived to have deteriorated, and the decisions made by those in charge, who focus on efficiency, oblivious to values and identities. The second part of the book explores the narrative dimensions of values-based organizations. "Narrative capital" is a precious resource in many of these organizations, particularly through periods of crisis and change. But problems can also be caused if the second and later generations after the foundations continue to use the original narrative without enough innovation. Finally, the book discusses the gaps – the surpluses and misalignments – between people, their ideals and the organizations and how these can be managed. The book is written for academics, students and others interested in the role of values and ideals in organizations – economists, sociologist, business scholars, theologians and philosophers.

Luigino Bruni is Full Professor in Political Economy, Department of Law, Economics, Politics and Modern languages, University LUMSA, Rome, Italy.

T0347543

Economics and Humanities

Series Editor: Sebastian Berger, *University of the West of England (UWE Bristol), UK.*

The *Economics and Humanities* series presents the economic wisdom of the humanities and arts. Its volumes gather the economic senses sheltered and revealed by some of the most excellent sources within philosophy, poetry, art and storytelling. By re-rooting economics in its original domain, these contributions allow economic phenomena and their meanings to come into the open more fully; indeed, they allow us to ask anew the question, "What is economics?". Economic truth is thus shown to arise from the human rather than the market.

Readers will gain a foundational understanding of a humanities-based economics and find their economic sensibility enriched. They should turn to this series if they are interested in questions such as the following: What are the economic consequences of rooting economic truth in the human? What is the purpose of a humanities-based economics? What is the proper meaning of the "oikos", and how does it arise? What are the true meanings of wealth and poverty, gain and loss, capital and productivity? In what sense is economic reasoning with words more fundamental than reasoning with numbers? What is the dimension and measure of human dwelling in the material world?

These volumes address themselves to all those who are interested in sources and foundations for economic wisdom. Students and academics who are fundamentally dissatisfied with the state of economics and worried that its crisis undermines society will find this series of interest.

The Ethics of Economic Responsibility
Ralf Lüfter

The Economics of Values, Ideals and Organizations
Luigino Bruni

For more information about this series, please visit: www.routledge.com/Economics-and-Humanities/book-series/RSECH

The Economics of Values, Ideals and Organizations

Luigino Bruni

Routledge
Taylor & Francis Group

LONDON AND NEW YORK

First published 2021
by Routledge
2 Park Square, Milton Park, Abingdon, Oxon OX14 4RN

and by Routledge
52 Vanderbilt Avenue, New York, NY 10017

Routledge is an imprint of the Taylor & Francis Group, an informa business

© 2021 Luigino Bruni

British Library Cataloguing-in-Publication Data
A catalogue record for this book is available from the British Library

Library of Congress Cataloging-in-Publication Data
Names: Bruni, Luigino, 1966- author.
Title: The economics of values, ideals and organizations / Luigino Bruni.
Description: Milton Park, Abingdon, Oxon; New York, NY: Routledge, 2021. | Series: Economics and humanities | Includes bibliographical references.
Identifiers: LCCN 2020055254 (print) | LCCN 2020055255 (ebook)
Subjects: LCSH: Values–Economic aspects. | Economics–Moral and ethical aspects.
Classification: LCC HB72 .B775 2021 (print) | LCC HB72 (ebook) | DDC 174/.4–dc23
LC record available at https://lccn.loc.gov/2020055254
LC ebook record available at https://lccn.loc.gov/2020055255

ISBN: 978-0-367-76261-2 (hbk)
ISBN: 978-0-367-76262-9 (ebk)

Typeset in Times New Roman
by Deanta Global Publishing Services, Chennai, India

This book is dedicated to Chiara Lubich, who taught me what ideals and charisms are.

Contents

Introduction

> When a truly original genius makes its appearance in the world, people make haste to get rid of it. To achieve this goal, they have two methods. The first is elimination. In the event of failure, they adopt the second method (which is much more radical and hideous): exaltation, putting it on a pedestal and transforming it into a "god".
>
> (Lu Xun, *An Introduction to the Sayings of Confucius*: 2016, Adelphi, Milan)

To understand the culture and nature of our capitalism, we need to look at what is going on inside *organizations*, where we spend most of our lifetime. It is necessary to look at all kinds of organizations, including those driven by non-material or non-monetary incentives, that are much more frequent and relevant than we usually think. Economics knows non-profit organisations, but analyzes with the same tools used for all kind of firms and organizations. We need a specific reflection on institutions driven by "ideal" forces, that are not understood if seen throughout the eyes of mainstream economics.

This small book is dedicated to the so-called VBOs, i.e. *values-based organizations* (or values-driven organizations or charismatic organizations), namely organizations, institutions and communities inspired by ideals, a mission or "vocation" related in various ways to the intrinsic motivations of those who promote it. From Freud onwards, we know the ambivalent nature of the ideal. The ideal is the main pushing and driving force of history, but often the ideal becomes also the main source of guilt and frustration of individual and community, if the gap between the real and the ideal is interpreted as failure and sin. This radical ambivalence of ideals is one of the main hermeneutic keys of this volume.

In the sociology of religion there is also another word that I will use often in this book: *Charism*, that in the Bible and in Christianity expresses a spiritual *gift* received by a given person that often generates a *charismatic* organization, community or movement (Bruni and Sena, 2012; Bruni and Smerilli, 2009, 2015).

The ideal motivation, mission, vocation or charism inspiring VBOs takes various forms. It can be embodied in the kind of activity they perform (charity, care, philanthropy…), in the motivations at the origin of their foundation, in their different way of doing business, i.e. management, governance, leadership inspired by values other than mainstream organizations. These characteristics are often co-present and intertwined in a VBO, even though to different degrees and in different combinations – it is hard to imagine, in practice, an ideal motivation of the founders that does not generate a consistent governance and organization culture. For this charge of ideality, VBOs are more subject than other organizations to some typical relational and motivational dynamics that will be described in this book.

At the same time, the analysis used in this book does not apply *just* to VBOs, because characteristics of charismatic leadership and the dynamics that we will explore can be found also in family businesses, or even ordinary for-profit companies in which the founder or the leader plays an essential role. Similar dynamics can also occur in political parties, academic communities and scientific schools. The field of application of this discourse is therefore at once narrow (charismatic/ideal membership and leadership) and wide (many forms of organizations). The intuition at the core of the book, in particular in Chapter 1, is that VBOs depend chiefly on the presence of *conformist* members for their success, who comply perfectly with the objectives and strategies of the founder/leader. At the same time, for their middle-long run survival and growth, such organizations depend chiefly on *non-conformist* creative members, with the capacity for innovation. The interplay between conformist and non-conformist members in VBOs is one of the pillars of this chapter. In particular, a special emphasis will be placed on a special form of "resource curse", which often affects organizations with a strong and talented founder or leadership (Antoci, Bruni, Rossi and Smerilli, 2020). This curse may arise because the leader, in order to maximize the organization's efficiency in the initial phases of the development of the institution, tends naturally to select and reward (in many ways) *conformist* members and, consequently, discourages non-conformist ones, because at the moment of the foundation he/she does not like the freedom and autonomy of creative and non-conformist members in the organization. Such a human resources policy works in the first period and allows for the huge growth of the organization but becomes a poverty trap in the post-foundation period, during which creative members would have been essential in the development and continuation of the organization, and they are no longer there because they are discouraged and disincentivized in the first stages. This form of "leadership curse" becomes more probable and severe, the stronger and more charismatic the founder is. In fact, the crucial moment in a VBO arrives when the charismatic founder leaves. When the leader is active in the organization, he/she is the most important source of innovation: In this case, the best results in the organization can be achieved when the members of the organization do not question the leader, but instead follow his/her inspiration and instructions. We'll see that in the long run this kind of behaviour results in a lack of creativity and innovation. In particular, these dynamics occur when charismatic leadership transform organizational culture into a sort of "cult". The following pages arise from the explicit intention to offer tools for analyzing the typical organizational phenomena of the movements, both for those communities that have already been hit by illnesses and neuroses for some time, and above all, for those who are in the early stage of success and development. Because the big crises begin when everything speaks of success and development, if leaders are not endowed with wisdom to change when nobody wants to. For such phenomena we'll use the metaphor of "auto-immune disease".

Charisms continue in history the function of biblical *prophets*. Due to their vocation, the prophets are often found in a vital and necessary tension with the institutions and hierarchy. Without prophets, the promised land remains just a utopia, institutions become structures to dominate and exploit the weakest, the world no longer knows how to listen to the voice that speaks and the spirit that blows. Similarly, it happens for charisms, which are an essential dimension for raising the spiritual and moral quality of the world, and for looking upwards. When charisms are lacking in communities, organizations and people, or are silenced and marginalized, the beauty, lightness, spiritual strength of life in common fades away, and we begin to settle for sad and small goals.

Charisms extend to the world the horizon of all, even of those who do not believe in charisms or consider them harmless for people left at the infant stage of existence. In other words, without prophets, life on Earth would become very sad and perhaps impossible. And the poor would never be loved and respected, at most settled in refugee camps or in special facilities.

Charisms have never been a purely religious affair (Bruni and Sena, 2012). They are much more. Their job is to make the Earth more beautiful, not just religions and churches. Yesterday and today their water is that of public fountains, not only that of holy water and baptismal fonts. But today, much more than yesterday, many charismas live outside the visible boundaries of churches and religions, yet they continue to carry out their essential function of *charis*, prophecy and beauty. At the same time, yesterday and today very delicate and often dangerous social, ethical and spiritual dynamics stem from charisms, as their immense strength can be oriented, almost always without intentionality, for purposes that are harmful to people and to the very charismatic realities. For that reason, we'll see that the renewal of a charismatic community is as crucial as it is unlikely, because the institutions that are born of the charism to keep it alive and serve it end up becoming the final goal of the movement itself, from means become ends.

One important and crucial element, that inspires the whole book, is the *unintentional* nature of the perverse dynamics of VBOs: Neither the founders nor the most motivated and innovative members want the decline of the ideals that they often create. On the contrary, they use all their strength to rekindle the charism and to make it bear copious fruits. But, as is well known in history and widely studied in the sociology of religions and charismatic movements, the most natural temptation of any reality born of an ideal is *ideology*. In fact, this book can also be seen as a discourse on the *nature of ideology*. The transformation of the ideal into an ideology, that is a version of the biblical *idolatry*, is always possible until a community maintains the gap between its ideal and its actual experience, and therefore between the charism and the institutions shaped to incarnate it and live it. But it falls into idolatry when this gap leaps, and the ideal ends up coinciding with the works it generates. We'll see that idolatry and ideology are two sister words. A charism starts declining when it turns into an ideology, namely when the charism becomes the explanation of all reality. It becomes fully self-referential. Distinguishing the *ideals* from the *ideology of the ideals* is a decisive, delicate but unavoidable process for saving the charism from itself.

In the development of our discourse, we will claim in various ways that a charismatic community or movement remains alive as long as they put their inhabitants in the conditions – always demanding and never predictable – of being able to embellish, renovate, paint and even remould its original charismatic work. As long as a community grants its members the possibility of being able to creatively restructure the original "building", to be able to exercise what the economist Joseph A. Schumpeter called "creative destruction", the quality of life of this community remains high and dynamic. When this option and freedom are lacking, the dominant notes become the sadness and death of creativity. Beyond this possibility, risky and vital, the envisageable scenarios are either the destruction of the building or the sale of the building to other owners and therefore the loss of one's identity and history. The VBOs that have shown themselves alive and long-standing are those with plural deltas and with many streams. Monolithic, compact and monotonous estuaries have a short life span. Biodiversity is the law of life, of every life under the sun.

The book is divided into three parts. The first chapter – *Organizations* – is about the relationship between persons and organizations, individuals and governance. We will begin our reasoning by analyzing, in the first chapters, some phenomena common to all organizations, communities and companies, i.e. the management of vulnerabilities in relationships and the role of incentives, especially in relation to the essential virtue of loyalty. Then, we will enter the VBOs territory, to see what specific aspects the motivations of their members take on in these "special" organizations, how to retain the most motivated people, who are generally the first to complain and threaten to leave when they perceive that the ideals of the organization have deteriorated, also as a result of decisions made by those in charge, who focus on efficiency, oblivious to values and identities.

The second part is an analysis of the *narrative* dimensions of VBOs. Communities, associations, movements, institutions and businesses live through many forms of capital. One of these is *narrative capital*, a precious resource in many organizations, which becomes essential in times of crisis and in the great changes on which the quality of the present, the possibility of the future and the blessing or curse of the past depend. It is the patrimony – namely *munus*/gift of the fathers – made of stories, writings, sometimes poems, songs and myths. It is a real *capital* because, like all capitals, it generates fruits and future. If the ideals of the organization or community are high and ambitious, as they happen to be in many VBOs, their narrative capital is also great. It is a precious resource during the first difficulties, when telling each other the great episodes of yesterday gives courage to continue to hope, believe and love today. But, we'll see, very soon begins a sort of *parasite* syndrome, because the second and later generations after the foundation will continue to use the original narrative without enough innovation. This rent-disease is a serious pathology of VBOs, difficult to heal because is not-intentional.

Finally, the book ends with Chapter 3 discussing the *surpluses* and *misalignments* between people and their organizations. The issues discussed in this last chapter include the following: what are the typical characteristics of the management of these surpluses in the various phases of the life of the person and the organization? How do they handle surplus as a young person, and how do they do it when they are old? How can we save biodiversity to ensure new life? How can we preserve multi-dimensional vocations today?

We will face these and other vital challenges. Most of the questions will remain unanswered. The gaps between the questions raised and the answers proposed is the land where new research can flourish tomorrow.

Rome 2, June 2020

1 Organizations

On gratuitousness

Gratuitousness is the main taboo of capitalism. It is feared as the greatest danger, because if it were let to run freely in the territories of capitalism, they would be infected and its "poison" would cause its death, or – by the same token – it would turn it into something substantially different. It is difficult to see the taboo of gratuitousness in our economy (and society) because another taboo conceals it, namely the recognition of its existence. In order to understand the profound relationship between gratuitousness and capitalism, we must violate this first taboo by merely starting to talk about it.

According to an important anthropological tradition, the origin of civilization is deeply connected to two words: *Violence* and the *sacred*. Even the Bible begins human history outside of Eden with Cain's fratricide. The death of the meek and righteous Abel becomes the first price of the foundation of human civilization. Founding myths of other cities (e.g. Rome) narrate similar cases of violence and murder (Bruni, 2019).

Communities had to learn how to manage people's violent impulses, to prevent their own destruction. The creation of taboos must be included among the tools to regulate and control violence, in order to prevent it from becoming emulative, recurrent and explosive. Communities have paid a heavy price for these tools, as they applied to persons and actions leading to forms of discrimination and, more often than not, actual persecution of those who were subject to taboos (women, lepers, the poor, the sick, entire peoples).

The relationship between a community and its taboos shows a radical *ambivalence*. On the one hand, a taboo *is all that you have to avoid*, all you cannot touch, against which you should get immunized not to become contaminated and infected by its spirit (the *mana*). Furthermore, the words associated with taboos should *not be pronounced*. The land of a taboo cannot be crossed. Communities have changed; they have died and been resurrected according to the rhythm of the creation, violation and elimination of taboos. Even if by completely different modes, the same ancestral rhythm of the Earth keeps appearing in our history.

Likewise, the content of taboos carries a fatal and strong attraction, by developing some invincible traits in people: A taboo cannot be violated, but (and because) we profoundly wish to do so, the desire for vengeance on Cain ("whoever finds me will kill me") produces his "mark" ("lest any who found him should attack him"): Genesis 4:14.

His words are banned, but the temptation to pronounce them is strong. For example, based on what Freud calls "the taboo on the rulers", kings cannot be touched by their subjects: A ban that aims to counter the deep passion-desire present in members of the community to kill the kings and rulers.

Objects, animals and people considered taboo also have a dual characteristic: They cannot be touched, nor can they be eliminated. The goal of the use of taboos is not their disappearance, since, if taboos were to disappear, the impassable border would also be gone with it, the community would be contaminated, and so it would fall exactly into the "sin" that the taboo was meant to avoid. The taboo and its marks must therefore be very visible; everyone must be able to recognize the totems.

We can understand a lot about how capitalism works and, in general, about economics, if we take its taboos of gratuitousness seriously. The relationship between gratuitousness and the market encompasses the anthropological traits of taboos.

First, we find the original violence.

Traditional or pre-commercial communities hinged upon two original and distinct principles: *Hierarchy and gift*. Hierarchy was the instrument for the management of power, while gift regulated reciprocity in families, within clans and communities. The advent of the market took place *after the killing of the gift*, which must die in order to create the contract and commercial exchange in its place, which are characterized so as *not to be* a gift, not to be gratuitousness. Market economy does not question the hierarchy; conversely, it radicalizes it – to the extent that capitalist enterprises are also the main place, along with the armies, where hierarchy continues to play a significant and, after all, socially accepted role in the age of democracies.

At the origin of the market, however, there is a sort of primordial violence on gratuitousness-gift (even if it is neither perceived nor told as such by its protagonists). Even Cain's violence is linked to gift and to the economy. God did not accept his gifts, a denial that generated violence on Abel, the elimination of the fragile brother, who knew how to make gifts.

Gratuitousness is always as fragile and vulnerable as Abel; it is exposed to abuse. However, Cain is also the patron of trades and the founder of the first city, which is named after his son (Enoch). In addition, its very name has a strong assonance with the verb *qanah*: To buy.

Furthermore, in the Book of Genesis, the word "profit" (*bècà*) makes its appearance in the scene of Joseph being sold into slavery, again, by his brothers (37, 28). The fraternity of the gifts is denied by the appearance of profit. In Rome, *numus* (currency) was the non-*munus* (gift). In modernity, at the heart of the founding myth of political economy, "the invisible hand", we find the argument that the engine of the wealth of nations is not the "benevolence" or gratuitousness of traders, but their personal interests (Adam Smith, *The wealth of nations*, 1776). The *visible* hand holding gifts was replaced by the *invisible* hand of the market, which is not the Providence during ancient times, because its nature lies in the absence of gifts.

Neither can gratuitousness be profaned in the market, but it must be visible and well in sight. The boundary around its territory coincides with the very limits of the market: The land of what is freely given starts where that of the market, the contract and incentives ends. Gratuitousness begins beyond the company's gates, after we have done the shopping and gone home. Everyone should see it, everyone must understand it without any complex speeches: It is enough to identify its signs and its totems: Workplace time cards, the duration of lunch breaks, the management of overtime and especially the *language*. The words of taboos cannot be uttered: Woe to those who say the word gift or gratuitousness and its synonyms in the ordinary course of business.

Nevertheless, as happened in some totemic civilizations, there are some specific times when the untouchable subject of taboos can and should be mentioned, sacrificed, ritually consumed, in order to seize its mysterious and terrible force. Hence, in business assemblies gift is evoked, pronounced, consumed and then put back in its inviolable tabernacle the next day. We organize employee volunteer initiatives, social dinners to help the poor, to provide organized and regulated activities within the reassuring confines of the rules, limited to that carefully controlled time. These *donuncoli*, domesticated gifts, managed and controlled, are the new voodoo dolls, resembling the real person (gift-gratuitousness) with the hope of handling it and subjecting it to witchcraft.

Then, what are the deep reasons for the fear that gratuitousness causes in the capitalist economy, to make it the primary taboo? The first reason lies, again, in its appeal. Even in the case of gratuitousness, like all taboos, prohibition stems from a deep desire. We wish for nothing more than gift: We yearn for it, it makes us feel alive, it is our profound vocation. Moreover, if the economy is life, the charm of the gift (given and received) is strongly perceived, and even more so in the economic life.

However, nothing is more outrageous than gift; nothing is free anymore. It is everywhere and it is free, but in the economic field its effects would be particularly devastating. Because it would break the rules of contracts, it would undermine the hierarchy. If companies accepted and embraced the register of the gift-gratuitousness, they would find themselves with people who are unmanageable, unpredictable and capable of actions that cannot be controlled by hierarchies and incentives, because they would be truly free. They would have to deal with workers who would follow their intrinsic motivation, working beyond the limits of the contract, which are too tight and small to contain the overflowing power of gift. They would be faced with people who would not fit in the organization charts, the job descriptions, people who would bring much more life and, therefore, much more confusion and noise with them – as it happens with living things. If company managers recognized this gift as such, if it made them grateful towards their colleagues and employees, that free reciprocity and those strong *bonds* would be created in businesses that are the typical fruits of gifts, that are recognized, accepted and reciprocated. It would change the hierarchy, which would become fraternal and therefore fragile, vulnerable, exposed just like the meek Abel; but fragility and vulnerability are the great enemies of capitalist enterprises and their immune cultures. To avoid the risk of recognizing gifts and the generation of strong ties, business culture and governance just react by denying it: This is how the taboo of gratuitousness is reborn and strengthened every day. Companies and markets will protect themselves from gratuitousness to protect themselves from their own death.

But there is also something else to say. In recent years, the taboo of gratuitousness has left the economy and large companies to move progressively and quickly to civil society, to non-profit organizations, associations, movements and communities. The taboo is expanding and the house of gratuitousness on Earth is becoming increasingly more cramped. Management techniques and tools, which until recently belonged exclusively to large companies and banks, are now entering many areas of civil society. The real – almost always invisible albeit very high – price of the entry of capitalist management into civil organizations, movements and communities is the gradual elimination of these places of free gifts. So, paradoxically, the taboo of gratuity is created right in the heart of the realities that were born from and for gratuitousness.

The spirit of differences

The beauty of social life mainly depends on the game and the interweaving of differences. The Earth is not only beautiful for the variety of butterflies and flowers. There is much beauty generated by differences in the ways and forms of doing economy, enterprise or banking. Even greater is the beauty that comes from differences between people, from the encounter of their different talents, from the dialogue between their motivations.

Many civil "works of art" that continue to beautify our common ground were carved out of motivations that were greater than economic incentives, of some "because" that was deeper than the monetary "why". If their founders had obeyed the iron law of business plans, today we would not have all the institutions for the disabled that have loved our special children, nor the thousands of cooperatives born from the desire for life and future of our fathers, mothers and grandparents. These works that flourished because of greater ideals endured over time and beyond ideologies, crossing through the centuries. They sprang from great motivations that have been able to generate considerable, long-lasting and fertile outcomes. Economic and civil life, human life, feels an extreme need for all human resources, as well as the deepest of motivations. Economy reduced to pure economics is lost and is no longer capable of generating life or good economy.

One of the most radical trends of the *humanism of immunity* underlying contemporary capitalism is the need to control, curb and normalize the deepest motivations of human beings, especially those that are inherent, where our gratitude and freedom have their roots. As a matter of fact, when we activate our passions, ideals and our spirit, sometimes it happens that our ways of behaviour go beyond the control of organizations. Our actions become unpredictable because they are free, and therefore they put protocols and *job descriptions* in crisis. They cause crisis, especially in management that – because of its tasks and nature – has to make organizational behaviour controllable and predictable. To be able to handle many different people and direct them all towards the basic goals of the company, it is necessary to implement a strong homogenization and standardization of behaviour, so that they become incapable of creativity (that all of them would like, by their words). Intrinsic motivations are more powerful and, therefore, more destabilizing. We disengage from the cost-benefit calculation and become able to do things just for the *inherent* happiness of the action. We would not have scientific research, poetry, a lot of art or true spirituality without intrinsic motivations, as we would not have many businesses, communities and organizations, arising from the passions and ideals of the founders and living because and insofar as someone continues to work not only for money. All true creativity has an essential need for intrinsic motivation. But – as we see every day, tragically – intrinsic motivation is also at the root of the worst human behaviours.

Here is the reason why the modern spirit, in particular the economic spirit, chose to settle only for the instrumental or extrinsic motivations

– fearing the potentially destabilizing effects of the great human motivations. Therefore, we have let democracy manage the public game of differences and identities, but we expelled it from businesses. And so our organizational culture seeks to turn human motivation into all the various incentives to reduce the many "because"-s into a single, simple "why". We have thus reduced the wounds (vulnerability) inside our businesses, but we have also reduced the blessings (welfare).

Incentives have become a great tool for controlling and managing "reduced" people who are underpowered in their many motivations, in order to align them with the goals of organizations (the *incentivus* was the wind musical instrument that gave the tune for the instruments of the orchestra, the trumpet that *incited* the troops to battle, the *enchanting* flute of the snake-charmer). So, economics and managerial sciences have come to settle for the less powerful motivations of humans – even when they try to manipulate them by promising new recruits a paradise that they cannot and do not want to give. This is also a price of modernity.

The operation of motivational levelling is dangerous everywhere, because the "one-dimensional man" does not work well anywhere and, most importantly, is not happy. Dropping out the deepest, generative and free motivations results in disastrous consequences for the organizations born and fuelled by ideals, charismas, passions – the so-called VDO-s (values-driven organizations). These "different" organizations have a basic need to involve a share, however small, of workers, executives and founders with intrinsic motivation, endowed with a "genetic code" that is different from the one assumed and implemented by the dominant management theory. These people are active in social enterprises and civil, religious communities, in many non-governmental organizations (NGOs), spiritual and cultural movements, in the world of environmentalism, critical consumption and human rights; but often we find them also among the founders of family businesses, and in much of the "normal" economy of craftsmen, small businessmen, cooperatives and ethical and territorial financing.

We would not have these organizations and communities without the presence of these "yeast" type of people who are creative, generative and often destabilizing in terms of the established order, as they are "inner-driven", namely the bearers of a "charisma" that pushes them to act in obedience to their *daimon*. These workers of an intrinsic motivation have two principal motivational marks. On the one side, they are little motivated by the economic incentives of management theory and respond poorly, or not at all, to the external sound of the charmer flute, since they love to hear other, internal melodies instead. At the same time, they are infinitely sensitive to the ideal size of the organization that they have founded or where they work; not only for economic, but rather for identity, idealistic and vocational reasons.

Management of people with intrinsic motivation is crucial when these organizations go through times of crisis and conflict, caused by a generational or leadership change, for example, or the death and succession of the founder. These moments – that are delicate ones in every organization – are crucial to the VDOs, because of the most typical and all too common error: Not understanding the very petitions and complaints coming from the most motivated members. As a matter of fact, if those who manage or accompany a VDO as consultants do not recognize the value of these deeper motivations, that are different from incentives, not only do they not reach the goal they hoped for, but they further worsen the crisis of these people and the organization.

When the ideal's quality is at stake, usually the first to complain are the ones who are more interested in the quality that is being lost. However, if directors and managers interpret this type of protest merely as a cost, and therefore do not accept it and reject it, the first ones to quit are the best ones – as I tried to show in some studies carried out together with Alessandra Smerilli. Since these people are practically insensitive to incentives but very sensitive to the ideals-values dimension, they are willing to give much more than their contract states, granted that it is "worth it", as long as the values they have invested in heavily are kept alive and recognized. There are people, even within firms, who assign such a high value to the symbolic values and ethical principles that inspire their work, for which they are willing to do (almost) everything. But as soon as they realize that the given organization is becoming (or has become) something other, all the intrinsic reward that they drew from their work-activity is dramatically reduced; in some cases it is even undermined (or becomes negative). This is also an expression of the ancient intuition (which dates back at least to St. Francis of Assisi) that real gratuitousness does not come at a *zero* price (free) but at an *infinite* price.

Crisis management in VDOs is a real art, and it requires leaders' ability to distinguish the different types of discomfort and protest, and to know how to appreciate and use the protest that rises above all from those who are the guardians and bearers of the values and ideals of the organization. The neo-managerial ideology, however, is getting increasingly more flattened onto a single motivational register. It does not have the categories to understand the different types of protest, and so it is unable to recognize that behind a threat of abandonment, a cry of love may be hidden.

People with intrinsic motivations usually also have great resilience and great fortitude in adversities. They manage to last long in a state of protest, preferring to stay albeit in protest (Albert Hirschman defines protesters who will not quit as loyal). People with strong intrinsic motivations quit and leave only when they lose hope that the organization can recover the lost ideals, and sometimes their quitting itself becomes the last message to arouse extreme revision in the leaders. Hence, it is understandable that a VDO is wise if it knows how to keep people loyal, giving citizenship rights to their protest, valuing it and not considering it as a cost or friction.

Biodiversity within organizations is going through a significant decline, and motivational levelling produces growing discomfort and *malaise* even in the heart of capitalism. And those who love and live in ideal-driven communities and organizations have to defend and preserve the now endangered intrinsic motivations. Maybe you can keep running for years in a multinational without giving space to ideal motivations, but the VDOs die soon if we reduce all our passions to sad incentives.

The courage to think of the orchard

The creation of many companies and organizations aims to seize a market opportunity, to respond to a need, to provide a service. In other cases, however, they are the emanation of personality, passions, ideals of one or more persons, who utter and embody the most solemn words, along with the largest projects of their lives in their organization. One name for such organizations is value-based-organizations (VBOs) or charismatic organizations (CHAOs).[1]

The world is full of these different types of organizations and communities and many of the finer and higher things of life take place within these organizations and communities, where people's motivations become projects, the projects make history, a history embellished with many colours and flavours. These entities, if they want to last beyond the life of the founder, have a vital need for creative and innovative members. But once these organizations and communities start growing and developing, those who generated them eventually create governance structures that prevent the emergence of new creativity, and so they pave the way for their own decline. This is a fundamental law of motion of history: The first creativity that generates organizations and communities, at some point, starts building up inside the antibodies to protect itself against new creativity and innovations that would be essential for them to survive longer. It is a severe autoimmune disease affecting many organizations and communities.

Its root lies in the mismanagement of the fear of losing the originality and the specific identity of the founder's "charisma". For fear of dilution, contamination or degradation of the original purity of the organization-community's mission, people with greater creativity are discouraged because they are perceived as a threat to its identity. Thus, instead of emulating founders in their creative capacity, there is a focus on imitating the forms through which this capacity emerged and developed. The immutable core of the original inspiration is confused with the historical organizational form that it took in the early stages of foundation, and it is not clear that the salvation of the original inspiration stems from changing these forms, in order to remain faithful to the essence of the original nucleus. Therefore, everything ends up trying to become immutable, to remain unchanged and to wither.

There are many symptoms of this illness. The most visible one is the emergence of a general inability to attract new generative and valuable people. The most profound one is the famine of *eros*, of passion and desire, which manifests itself in a collective organizational sloth. If the desires and passions of the new members are oriented towards the historical forms in which the founder has embodied their desires and passions, they end up longing for the fruits of the tree, not for the tree that generated them. Those who govern an organization and want it to survive over time should say to their creative and young people: "Do not desire the fruits generated yesterday that are fascinating you today. Be a new tree".

The only real chance for a tree that has borne fruit to continue to live and bear fruit is to become an orchard, a wood, a forest. Exposing itself to the wind and accommodating bees among its branches that may spread its seeds and its pollen in the soil, generating new life. Saint Francis is still alive after centuries because his charisma was generative of hundreds and thousands of new Franciscan communities, all equal and all different, all of Francis' and all expressions of the genius of the many reformers who, through their creativity, have made that first tree become a fruitful forest.

There are no guarantees that the creativity of the new arrivals will bring the same fruits the founder did, and that anyone who tastes them recognizes the same taste of the first fruits or finds them even better – "you will do things bigger than me". Certainty, however, is death, unless you have the courage to face this vital risk. A VBO can die because of infertility, but it can also die because it turns into something that has nothing to do with the VBO and the ideals of the founder – as is the case with far too many works of religious orders taken over by companies whose sole purpose is profit or income and have no relationship whatsoever with the first charismatic DNA. In every field, there is a path to embark on to be able to continue the dream of founders in faithful creativity, but it is in that mestizo territory of venture, trust, wisdom of governance, an alchemy always unpredictable with regard to its final outcomes.

The culture and the choices of governance have a specific responsibility in these crucial stages, and most certainly in relation to the transition from the founding generation to the next, but also when time calls for profound and brave changes. At the origin of the autoimmune disease, there is almost always the leaders' fault in using the most innovative members only for executive and functional tasks, not allowing them to flourish and develop their talents. Indeed, here is where the heart of the disease (and its cure) stands. In the early days of the foundation, the days of pure creativity that may last for decades, the VBOs attract excellent people, bearers of talents and "charisma" in synergy with the ones of the founder. The governing wisdom of the founder and/or his first employees lies in ensuring that creative people can flourish in their diversity, in not turning them into maids only at the service of the leader's charisma. As a matter of fact, if diversity is not appreciated and all the best talents are oriented towards a monistic culture, exclusively aimed at the development of the organization, the VBO ends up losing its biodiversity and fertility, and starts to decline.

Preventing and then treating this form of autoimmune disease is particularly difficult, because it is a pathological development of a process that was initially virtuous and indispensable for the birth, growth and success of the organization.

Hence, in the first stage of the founder's life, many VBOs experience what is perhaps the highest form of creativity that the human realm knows (the only one that can approach it is that of artists, which, by the way, is very similar). It is the season of pure, absolute, explosive and disruptive creativity. In order for this great creativity to be embodied in an institution, there is an essential need for people who realize, disseminate, consolidate and implement that creative energy, to channel the water of a new spring. All members are required to have some creativity, but we could call it a second-level one. It is the creativity expressed in the pursuit of forms, modes, means of implementation and embodying of the initial and original creativity in new geographic areas, in new and unprecedented economic sectors and areas. But the first and, in many cases, only virtue requested from the members of the VBO during this first stage is an absolute and unconditional fidelity to the original inspiration; all creativity and life force is subject to loyalty and put to its service as a subsidiary. Without this game of absolute loyalty and subsidiary creativity, many spiritual movements would not be born, nor the many communities that have made the world more beautiful and continue to improve it every day; just as many associations and social enterprises stemming and expanding from the *daimon* of the "prophets" of our time would not have appeared and grown.

Therefore, during this first phase, the creativity of the best members is directed by the governance of the organization towards their functions and for a "faithful" accountability. At the same time, as time passes, a growing number of new members are attracted, whose preferences are called "conformist" in economics literature. These persons derive happiness from aligning themselves with the dominant tastes, values and the culture in the group, because these are the values required and necessary at this stage of development. But when the founder or the founding generation leaves, these organizations and communities find themselves with members educated only to loyalty and creativity of the second level, while the organization in this new stage would need creativity of the first level, of the same nature of the founder, and of the one that had attracted them – no creative person is attracted to conformist imitators. This is how they fall into "poverty traps" that feed on themselves. On the one hand, for organization members it would be essential to have that generative and free creativity (of the first level) that had long been discouraged, and therefore, they are lacking it now. On the other hand, those "negative virtues" that were fundamental in the first stage of the organization eventually create a culture that is not really vivid or dynamic enough to catalyze new creative people, who would actually be rather essential to hope for a new spring. This is the main reason why the historical arc of the great majority of idealistic organizations follows the parable of their founders, and the generational change marks, as a matter of fact, the beginning of decline.

However, decline is not their only option, because the organizational autoimmune disease can be prevented, or at least taken care of, even though the only real medicine is to become aware of it when the process is still in its embryonic stage. Our history and the present tell us that sometimes movements flourish after the death of founders, communities are raised up by a generational shift and the tree does not die but multiplies in the orchard.

Do not give in to success

Organizations, communities and movements are living organisms: They are born, they grow, die, get sick and they are cured. There is a disease, that we called "autoimmune", which is particularly severe and difficult to cure, especially because its early symptoms are read as signs of success and health. As with all autoimmune diseases, the key factors for expanding and protecting a VBO, at some point, begin to infect the same social body which they had been nurturing for so long.

Let us think about the crucial issue of the structures and bureaucracies of VBOs. The rise of the organization, the works and institutions of its "charisma" are a sign of the fertility and strength of the experience. Their appearance is considered and hailed as a blessing and a great sign of fertility. Therefore, while, at the beginning, these structures were the fruit and the service of life, as they stemmed from encounters, needs and requests reaching the VBO from outside, at some point, they started being produced from inside, in order to envisage future needs and potential "questions". The central and auxiliary structures are created, evolve and develop internal bureaucracies that absorb an increasing amount of energy, human and spiritual forces that are harnessed to manage the structures generated by the first success. A bureaucratic class progressively develops and works full time. It grows in a hypertrophied way, which is interpreted as a strength and success of the movement-organization instead of being perceived as a sign of decline. Without structures and institutions, our ideals remain fleeting experiences, which are meant to leave no mark on history. However, as in the myth of Oedipus the King, the structures and the necessary bureaucracies may end up devouring the father who created them – and, as in the tragedy, despite unwillingness to do so or unawareness.

This law of "dusk starting at noon" can be found in many human organizations, especially the larger ones or those that are towering high above the others. We find it at work, especially in people with talent.

Writers or artists achieve their best thanks to the encounters and readings that nourish them in their early stage of training and development. It is at this point, however, that success may end up devouring talent. Writers stop feeding off of biodiversity, and protected and fostered by success, they begin to draw from themselves as they become self-consuming. They begin to browse through the books of other authors starting from the last page, searching for their own name among the references. As in any narcissism, they fall in love with their own reflection, until they drown in the lake of their own talent. They no longer feel the need to learn, to listen, to be asked questions by critics. This is where the decline of creativity begins, which initially does not look like a decline because it coexists with the increase in the number of fans, readers, recognition and consent. Nevertheless, it actually is the beginning of the sunset. You can only be saved at this point if you are able to see the start of decline and act accordingly, even though everyone and everything still speaks only of triumphs. If, however, you wait with this recognition until the moment when the sun is already down, then the process will be at a very advanced stage and often irreversible. As with other autoimmune diseases, the cure can come from outside the body: By yourself you can only see the sun of noon. Conversely, the others see more and much earlier than you, especially if they are your equals and not followers, and if they have the courage to take the risk of sharing (most likely) the fate of "Jiminy Cricket".

Something very similar happens to the bigger and better VBOs that are very similar to artists, people of genius – there are actually no organizations that could be more creative, sublime or exciting than the VBOs. The most important job of its founders and/or leaders is being able to see its self-destructive potential inside the culmination of success and behaving accordingly by making drastic and painful organizational decisions (for example, by discouraging the homogenization of its members, reducing distances between the leader and the group, fighting self-referentiality, not being willing to hear an echo of their own voice by their followers, promoting the autonomy of thought in people, etc.).

History tells us, however, that they almost inevitably do the opposite, and build organizations and hierarchical structures to lead all activities and the whole person of all people towards the strengthening and development of that success and acclaim.

How to escape from these sad outcomes that are self-generating and that no one should wish for? How can we not fall in love with our own success, and so condemn ourselves to infertility? Almost everything depends on the ability of the leaders not to make the commonest of all mistakes: Fatal reduction of identity. This mistake is usually made when the leaders, in order to direct all the moral energies of the members towards the goals of the organization, want a monopoly over their people. They create "one-dimensional" individuals, in terms of identity, thereby reducing – often unwittingly – the anthropological and motivational complexity. They forget that every person, especially those of quality are beyond the mission of the organization or movement, however great that is. This is where the true dignity of every person lies, which is greater than any paradise that is promised to them.

The importance of avoiding this error applies to every VBO, but it is decisive in the spiritual communities of the kind of people who have a dominant vocation, anchoring in the realm of "forever". Here the serious risk is not recognizing that the dominant identity is never the only axis of the person, and that its blossoming inside and outside the VDO depends on the interaction and the cross-fertilization of the many dimensions that make up its life. The paradox of gratuitousness is also to be found here: Ensuring that people can flourish and so enrich the organization, themselves, the world; no one should possess them, use them, eat them or even manipulate them, not even for the noblest purposes.

Every follower of a "charisma" springs up if they find their own way to respond to the vocation received, if they identify and cultivate their own "charisma" in what is preceding them. All those who are part of a VBO should try to avoid the mistake of "monopoly", but it is especially true for its leaders who should not support these trends, even when they are requested by the very people who seek a strong and all-encompassing identity; since if they support them, they soon find themselves surrounded by underpowered people, who keep losing their anthropological, moral and spiritual richness over the years. Obviously, these outcomes are non-intentional, and therefore very difficult to detect and treat – for this reason, it is important to tackle them.

When, however, this organizational generosity and chastity are lacking, people with vocations "work" for a few years, perhaps for decades, but they almost inevitably come to a moment of radical crisis, where they either quit to be saved or renounce to flourish in order to be saved – the world of religious orders and charismatic communities now offers us rich and growing empirical evidence for this.

At one point, life puts them at a crossroads: They should either take their life back in its entirety, pursuing new ways to flourish outside the VBO, or settle for a reduced life with no more *eros* and desires, even if this re-shaped life is accepted and interpreted as virtue and fidelity to themselves (and perhaps it also produces moral excellence for the individual – but rarely for the VBO). These organizational forms of chastity and gratuitousness are very rare and always sophisticated, because they require managers to be able to assist in developing latent and unforeseen vocations to touch new frontiers other than those already opened.

They should know how to not only appreciate and enjoy good orchestral performances of music that has already been written but let themselves be surprised by new works, new music and different dances. The VBOs that have lasted for many generations have been able to generate not only good interpreters but also many "composers" of new music, who wrote new melodies, often concerts and symphonies, using the first dominant motif offered to them, and have continued to make this world and heavens more beautiful.

Finally, there is a great message of hope in the possibility – as history, and also life tell us – that new concerts, dances and symphonies can flourish even inside the VBOs that are already suffering from autoimmune disease. First, because life is unpredictable and is more interesting than our descriptions of it, and so it happens that just like people, also organizations and communities can wake up one day and find themselves fully healed or getting better. Moreover, in human organizations there are always some vital areas, places and suburbs where some "prophesy" comes to the fore to those on the edges of the camp. But it is still possible to be saved because even in the hardest situations, there is always a third option. There are many people (I have known some myself) who – due to a mysterious but real gift – can have an experience that is similar to what Jesus proposed to Nicodemus: A man can be "born", even when he is "old". You may become adults and yet remain "children", you can grow well by staying in a VBO without becoming cynical or disenchanted. And so sometimes you become a stem cell capable of regenerating the entire organism. This third option is always possible, in all contexts, in all VBOs, in all the communities. Every day.

The freedom of the prophets liberates us

Generative communities and movements have always been those that put their members in a position to repeat the founder's experience in various forms: The same miracles, the same freedom, the same fruits. The history of Christianity is an eloquent demonstration of this: The fruitfulness of the Christian experience can be found in the thousands of communities and movements generated by the same origin that repeated the same experiences of the early days, over time and space, and have seen bread being multiplied, the lame walk and crucifixes raised. The charismatic experiences capable of a future have always been plural, pluralistic, orchards with many trees, gardens populated by hundreds and thousands of flowers, all equal and all different, growing from the same humus, with colours and scents that are similar or very different. The seed that takes the forms of the land where it grows, creating new personalities that enrich the earth.

Each member of an authentic charismatic community has, thus, his or her own features that radically differentiate him or her from other more common characters of our time (an employee, a fan of a writer, an activist of a humanitarian association). All these characters can often also be found in communities and charismatic movements, but in addition to them there are equally some very different ones. They are embodied by people who, getting in contact with an ideal-charisma, do not *encounter* something external to them, because they *meet* themselves. This experience is very common in spiritual movements, but we can also find it – in varying degrees – in some civil, political and cultural organizations. There are, as a matter of fact, men and women who, once they get in contact with a spirituality or an ideal, immediately feel a deep harmony between their more real, inner reality and the one they encounter. They are people in whom something of the same charisma approaching them is already alive, but they remain its "immune carriers" until they come in contact with the community where that charisma is at work and alive. When a young man begins to study chemistry and then starts to work in a company, he learns a profession, through his studies and work, that makes of him something different from what he was before. When, however, a young man encounters the charisma of Francis and feels a vocation, he does not become a Franciscan, because he is already one; in other words, he becomes what he already was. You can learn and acquire a profession, but you cannot learn a vocation: Van Gogh learned the techniques of painting, but he was already Van Gogh at the time.

This is the great mystery of charismas and all human vocations (the world is full of vocations). In the decisive encounter of their lives, these people have an "ontological" experience, one that happens on the level of existence, which is much deeper than the mere psychological and emotional dimensions. This means that a Jesuit does not receive the charisma of Ignatius or the other Jesuits, but he actually and mysteriously finds it in himself; he finds it alive and asleep in the "wine cellar" of the soul, where it has been waiting to be called by name. The encounter with a charisma lights up a latent but real dimension and generates a process of recognition: The person re-familiarizes with him/herself, and a new awareness and an unveiling of the self, so the world emerges from that decisive encounter. If it were not so, all the mystery and charm of vocations would disappear, we would all be meant to be followers of other people and external incentives, and true freedom and true donation would be precluded, as they arise only when one feels that following a charisma is following the best part of one's self, even if together with others and in a fundamental, defining relationship with the founder. On closer inspection, this game of becoming what one already is, the union between what is external and what is internal, can be found in every true love relationship, when upon meeting the other, we realize we have recognized someone who, mysteriously, has already been there somewhere in our lives, where he/she waited silently to be "seen". All this, and in an even more radical way, happens when it comes to collective authentic experiences of an ideal.

Two consequences can be derived from here. There have been, and there are many people on Earth who do not "light up" only because they have not had the opportunity to meet a person or a community capable of activating the deepest part in them. Secondly, there are always several encounters of a vocational dimension between people. Although for some (like a nun or an artist, for example) there may be a decisive encounter, this is never the only one, and the sure way to turn off the light on the main encounter is to put people in a position where they are not able to have further encounters of identity. The first and most important meeting does not become a prison if it does not become the only one.

This helps us understand that the experience of following a charisma (whether religious or civil) is a very delicate one. It always entails the risk that this ideal recognition between the person and the community may lead to a mutually narcissistic neurosis.

A crucial element is the management of disappointment. For those who encounter a charisma and set off on a journey, the experience of disappointment is inevitable, because no historical reality can be level with the ideal. The ideal of a community and the ideal within us had to be bigger than life; otherwise, they would have not "lit up" anything. Every good maturity is also a disappointment of the promises of youth.

If a disappointment is poorly managed and is not accepted, it produces two possible scenarios. Both of them are very dangerous: (a) the reduction of the ideal to reality and (b) the ideological interpretation of reality to make it coincide with the ideal. The first error is committed by the communities and people that, upon facing the first disappointments (especially collective delusions) reduce the ideal scope of the charisma and turn it into something more manageable and easy: YHWH gets reduced to the golden calf. The unavoidable outcome of this first error is the failure of this "new", resized ideal to attract high-quality people because when ideals are reduced, the excellent people can no longer be recognized. The second scenario is no less dangerous or harmful. It occurs when trying to prevent that people attracted by the great and necessarily non-real ideals come to the stage of disappointment, by building a real ideology. Instead of a common effort to accept and bridge the "gap" between the promises of an ideal and the possibilities of the real, they turn reality, any reality into an ideal, reinterpreting it every time, blaming the mismatch of the individual as responsible for the "gap". Disappointment as a natural and necessary part of the process of personal growth is therefore denied and drowned in the ideology, preventing the full thriving of members, who continue to be comforted and entertained, kept in an infantile condition. They are not disappointed since they are deceived. In the first scenario, the difference between ideal and reality vanishes by reduction (of the ideal); in the second one, it is eliminated for the sake of increase (of reality). However, what is not offered is the only real possibility for a positive overshoot of this decisive stage of all existence, and that is an education or training, preparing people for a coexistence with the gap, tending and processing the inevitable disappointments of adulthood, without dissolving either the truth of the ideal or that of reality.

It is understandable, then, that the ability of having a future of a collective reality born from an ideal-charisma essentially depends on how the relationship between founders, communities and the interpretation of charismas and individual "vocations" develop over time. The charismatic profile of a society is an expression and a continuation of the prophetic vocation, for which the Bible offers an ultimate type of grammar. The prophecy of the communities and charismatic movements, however, does not belong only to the founder or the community as a whole: Each person who received the same charisma embodies it, lives it and develops it by offering their own flesh. In each Franciscan, Gandhian, Dominican, Salesian, there is Isaiah, Jeremiah, Hosea revived, their words and their outrage are resurrected, as well as their criticism of the powers of every age, including our own. Moses, the greatest prophet lives again, as does his typical vocation of the liberator of an enslaved people from the pharaoh and his idols. Furthermore, the experience of prophecy is not reserved for the elite of intellectuals or professionals: Among the "prophets" that have loved and "lit me up", there are workers, peasants and women with only five grades of elementary school.

An ideal-driven organization lives well and makes its members and the world live well if it generates hundreds and thousands of Moses. But when communities and movements allow these moments of liberation only to their leaders, while all members are assigned the role of the people liberated and guided through the desert, it happens that vocations are turned off, the flowers wither, the prophetic power of the charisma is resized very much, or even too much. And the land of all loses brightness. There are few people on this Earth who are more beautiful than young people with a vocation, but there are very few experiences that are sadder than seeing those vocations fade away with adulthood.

Poverty re-creates the future

The big processes of change, those capable of regenerating the entire body and give way to a new spring, are never triggered and driven by the elites ruling at the stage of the emergence of a crisis. This dynamic is well known and extensively applied; therefore, it is also true for the entities that we have called communities and charismatic movements (as they were born from a charisma, which implies the gift of "a different gaze" on the world).

The most difficult but very important job of those who have to manage a living charismatic organization in decline is to understand – possibly at the right time – that the most significant process they should enable is the creation, by their own retiring, of the spaces of freedom and creativity that allow for the emergence of new dynamics and people who are different from those that they have generated. It is similarly important for them to be able to recognize these different people in the youngest son grazing the flock outside the house, in a child from a small town of Judah, in a brother cast away and sold as a slave. But when the ruling classes think, often in good faith, that they have to manage their own change, they almost unavoidably end up aggravating the illness they actually want to cure.

The entities that bloom from ideals are of two types: Those that arise from the start as organizations, and those that become organizations after being founded as a movement. In the first case, the one we have been calling VBOs, their ability to thrive and duration strongly depend on their inclination to create good structures, works and also robust, agile and efficient organizations. Here, if the founders' project does not turn into "works", it all ends with the first generation. As for the groups that are established as movements, what happens is exactly the opposite: A charismatic movement declines if after becoming an organization it is incapable of always reviving as a movement, by courageously renewing and dismantling the organizational forms that it has generated, and by resuming its journey towards new lands. Even in these entities, there comes a time for becoming an organization, but, if they get stuck at this stage, the prophetic power of the charisma starts fading away, and in some cases it disappears. The prophetic vitality of a charismatic movement is generating a lot of VBOs, without itself becoming a VBO – because in this case the organization devours the ideal's drive.

Once a movement turns into an organization, it can go through a new charismatic spring if in some marginal zone of the "kingdom" some creative minorities begin to rebuild the conditions for reviving the very "miracle" of the first foundation of the charisma: The same enthusiasm, the same joy and the same fruits. The process that leads these minorities towards becoming the majority is called *reform*, and it is the only possible cure for the collective entities that are stuck – still alive but no longer generative. Therefore, the momentum step for the renewal of a movement, which turned into an organization and wants to be a movement again, relies on the fact that its managers should understand the need to lay the foundations for new freedom and innovation that will lead others, not them, to re-launch a new charismatic stage, to become a movement again. That is why it is understandable that the crucial question is *how* to manage the process of renewal in those charismatic movement-communities that, notwithstanding the many difficulties, still have the desire and the potential for a future – and, thank God, there are still many of them.

The first general precondition is to try not to aggravate the illness while making efforts to cure it. When a charismatic group starts to envisage a decline, its leaders spontaneously begin to think that the cure is to change the structures and work on the organization itself. Thus, to reduce the weight of an organization that has grown too big over time (due to the autoimmune disorder we discussed in the Introduction), one continues to work and focus energies on the organizational aspects.

But if we look at the history and present of charismatic movements and communities, we realize that crises depend on a problem of "demand" (no more people attracted by a charisma) that was created years before by the errors of "supply" (too much structure, little creativity). When a movement goes through development, the need for strengthening the structures of the organization distances the most creative people of the peripheries, and they lose contact with the people and with the real dynamics of their own time, because they are increasingly more focused on the inside of the organization. So, faced with the demand for change, the government and the facilities react by continuing to look inward, creating new committees and offices, namely they keep looking at the structures only. A lot of hard work is done to simplify structures and so free up energy to give some time and breath back to people, without noticing that these same people – by their great majority – are no longer in a position to really start proclaiming the message again and attracting new vocations, because the charismatic message itself is in crisis and so is the issue of announcing and proposing it in a world where it seems no longer needed. There is a decisive process that should be carried out by involving and activating the key places for creativity and joining them to the borders of the empire. Certainly, all this is first and foremost gift (*charis*), but it is also organizational wisdom and profound, prophetic and transformational spiritual intelligence.

It is as if – to use a metaphor that may be flawed but perhaps not useless – a manufacturer of automobiles started to concentrate only on the supply side during the crisis of sales: Firing people, simplifying the organization, bundling, closing branches. However, if the problem is mainly on the demand side – the models offered today may be the ones that made it grow yesterday, but no longer meet the tastes of consumers – the real challenge is to invest resources in thinking about new models that would entrench the company's mission and tradition in the "market". If, however, people are liberated from administrative offices and move into the commercial space without renewing the "models", the first ones to experience frustration and failure will be the salespeople, who find themselves offering cars in which they no longer believe. A typical error committed during these phases of transition is, thus, thinking that the lack of attractiveness of the message affects only the outside of the community, and it is not widespread and deep inside it yet. It does not seem to be clear that without telling new and old stories that would rekindle the members and their vocations first, you will never be able to attract new people. Many new "evangelizations" happen when, while telling the good news to others, we also manage to hear it again and in a different way inside us. And so a new-old love story is reborn: A new *eros*, new desires, new generativity, new children. If you believe that the "illness" is curable by acting on the structural hypertrophy as a first step and then, later, on the "new models", the first ones to get discouraged will be the "dealers" themselves. During crises, moral energies are scarce, and it is crucial to decide what priorities to invest them in: Getting the temporal order and hierarchy of the interventions wrong is fatal. Because if you change the structures before rethinking the mission of a charisma, the real risk is that you get the direction of change wrong.

Charismatic movements and communities do not sell cars, but they also live and make others live well if and as long as they are able to actualize their charisma-message, translating it in the languages and desires of the present, and so attracting the best people today. Here again, the "new models" arise from the studies and the talent of the designers and the creative people, but first of all, they come from the visits to the new peripheries where there are new needs. Hence, they come from listening to the wishes of families and young people, from the body-to-body encounter with flesh and blood people. But the new sense of their own charisma and vocation is not found by looking – in a narcissistic way – within themselves, perhaps creating a new organizational structure dedicated to this. In these crises, there is generally plenty of technology, know-how or good engineers, but what is really missing is contact with the world, that has moved away too much over the years. Therefore, a charisma can only flourish by going out again to meet people in the streets, forgetting one's own organizations to deal with the wounds and sorrows of men and women of our days, and especially of the poor – distance from the poor is always the first sign of crisis of the charismatic entities. The "models" can and should be renewed, because a charisma is not a car, but an automaker company that, in order to live and grow has to be able to renew, change and interpret its mission creatively in the present time.

After the great flood, the Book of Genesis (ch. 11) tells the story of Babel. Saved by Noah, humanity, instead of listening to God's command and dispersing on Earth, got stuck, built a fortress, using a single language, without diversity. After the great crises, the temptation of Babel duly arrives: We are afraid, we protect ourselves, we tend to keep our own identity, we only look inward and lose biodiversity. Salvation lies in dispersion, in the many languages, in moving promptly towards new lands.

Betraying the ideal

Much more than interest, ideals are the force that pushes the world forward. Sometimes we are the ones that generate them in the brightest part of our soul. At other times, we are "called" by the ideals of others: One day we find out that they were already living inside us, just waiting to be lit up.

And so we begin the most sublime and generative types of adventures. In many cases, the greatest and most innovative ideals capable of generating a community arise from a person with a gift or a special *charisma* that can lead to collective experiences – at times very important ones, capable of transforming their own environment and their own time. Here the ideal is deeply intertwined with the personality of the "founder". It takes the founder's flesh; it grows and feeds off the founder's talents and character traits. This intertwining of the charisma and personality of founders is the source and strength of "charismatic communities". But there comes a time when, in order to continue its development without getting bogged down, a community must begin a long and complex process of distinguishing the "pearl" from the "field" that has kept it, to separate the personality of the founder from the "personality" of the charisma. As a matter of fact, if a charisma coincides with the talent of the person who embodies and announces it, it does not have the strength to go beyond the very person. However, when a charisma is rather excessive in relation to the person, and hence it creates communities and movements, this surplus becomes the source that feeds the community after its founder, precisely because it is bigger than him or her.

All significant charismas are greater than the charismatic person. Identifying this surplus, and so this "gap" between a charisma and the person being endowed with it, is a crucial endeavour, which all followers of a charismatic community are called to take on. Community, however, resembles a rather sophisticated collective work, as it requires the ability to understand that at the root of that specific community there was not only an ideal-charisma: There was also its *ideology*.

Every ideology has its own life cycle. Its birth takes place very early on. It begins with the idealization of some key figures in the community, the founder(s) or other people who have special talents or gifts. It then goes on from the ideal announced by the leader to the idealization of the person, so they gradually begin to lose touch with their own limits, errors, the typical shadows of the human condition. Myth and mythology surround leaders, while they make the person gradually more different and unique, with a kind of ethical and spiritual infallibility. As a result, the circle of people who work and interact with leaders slowly decreases, and the relationship between these few becomes increasingly asymmetric. Meeting or talking with leaders becomes a rare event, a ritual and mythical occasion. And the initial fraternity is gradually pushed to the background.

This is how the paradox is verified: Those who have received a charisma of fraternity and announce it often find themselves in the objective condition of not being able to live in the community that they have created. The first victim of ideology is, thus, the original community's fraternity. In the first, genuine and pure stage of ideals, fraternity is often the fundamental principle that involves everyone, including the founders and those who have prominent roles or responsibilities. When the community grows in size, some of these figures gradually disregard the game of fraternity and equality, and are wrapped in an exceptional status, which is almost never limited to the founder alone but includes his or her entire entourage. The stronger and the more exceptional the charismatic qualities of the founders are, the more likely and powerful the crisis of that fraternity and solidarity that once gave rise to the communities becomes. Communities founded by leaders with little spiritual talent are generally not very innovative, but they tend to remain more fraternal. Those that were born from great spiritual talents attract many more vocations but are much faster to produce ideologies that unhinge the original fraternity.

The second stage of ideology, which is a natural and logical follow-up to the first stage of the idealization of founders, is an overlap between the *charisma* embodied and announced by the founder and his or her *person*. Since there is always a necessary and special relationship between a charisma and the person who embodies it, it is very difficult for the founders of charismatic communities, and especially their followers, to be able to distinguish the proposed ideal from the ideological idealization of charismatic people. The exceeding of the experience of the ideal over the charismatic person is composed by charisma and ideology. But in the foundation stage, the strength of the leader's personality covers over the ideology, which actually often becomes an essential element for the growth and development of the first generation of the community – ideology is developed and empowered not only by founders but also by communities. The non-intentionality and good faith of the founders and their followers then makes the whole process even more complicated. However, when you switch from first to second and subsequent generations, it becomes essential to identify and distinguish the original charisma of the ideology that they have produced. If this delicate surgical operation is not attempted or if it is not successful, the ideology blocks the future development of a charisma, and often declares its end.

The crises of ideal-driven communities are produced by ideology, *not by the ideal*, and therefore can only be overcome by the elimination of ideology. But ideology acts primarily by making us blind to it because it dissimulates behind the ideal.

For this reason, ideologies hate crises and deny them in a radical manner for a long time, until it becomes too obvious (and when it is usually too late to attempt a cure). A crucial mark of ideology is, thus, the exclusion of the very possibility of crisis or decline from the horizon of future events. Everything is bathed in light, but much of this overall brightness is only the artificial light of ideology (true reality is always ambivalent). So when the ideology of charisma sends the charisma into crisis in the second or third generation, the community does not have the categories to devise, read, understand and overcome the crisis.

Therefore, the first step towards overcoming this crisis would be acknowledging that it is not the original message of the community (the charisma), which is in crisis, but the ideology that stemmed from it. Identifying the ideological nature of the crisis, however, is very difficult, because the ideological creation is intrinsic to the foundation stage, and extends to some choices, words and attitudes of the very founders. The cure from the crisis would require a freedom of interpretation of the charisma and its ideology, but it is precisely what the ideology has ruled out through its own development. Many charismatic communities cease to exist simply because of this. They could have been saved if they had tried, grabbing a scalpel, to penetrate into the living flesh, trying to remove the ideology to save the charisma.

And that is where different scenarios open up, of which the history of religions and ideal-driven movements is full. These scenarios are reminiscent of some dimensions present in the paradigms of two great Christological "heresies" of the first centuries of Christianity: Monophysitism and Pelagianism.

The "Monophysite" scenario (it recognizes only the *divine* nature, denying the human one) is the simplest and most common one: As people are unwilling or unable to admit the human and therefore ideological dimension in the person of the founder, they make no distinction between the original ideal and its ideology, and *everything becomes charisma*. And so all the words, all actions, all the episodes of the historical figure of the charismatic leader have the same foundational weight and the same nature. Ideology remains unseen, and the illness becomes incurable, since it spreads out unnoticed.

The other scenario is very reminiscent of *Pelagianism*, which was the great theological enemy of Saint Augustine. The spirit of Pelagius makes a new appearance when part of the community begins to think that they can "save themselves alone", imagining an exit from the crisis unleashed by the historical figure of the founder and his or her original charisma. They seem to glimpse a salvation but without a "saviour". Facing the discomfort that arises from the inability to rid the charisma of its ideology, the crisis is interpreted as a crisis of the charisma and so that of the figure of the founder (not of their ideology). It is put aside or used as a vague and distant ethical and symbolic reference, losing touch with the concrete and historical person. In these cases, the community/movement can also stay alive, but it becomes something substantially different from the first community.

Communities, however, that have managed to grow over time without falling into the new version of either of these two "heresies", entered confidently in the heart of the historical experience of the foundation, the founders and their myth, taking all the risks that such a delicate operation entails. They wanted to do it because at some point, often due to the intervention of authentic "reformers", they realized that there was no other scenario if they wanted to stay alive.

Ideal-driven and charismatic communities survive over time if every future generation has the courage to try and revive the ideal from the ashes of its ideology. But first they have to be able to identify it, understand it, accept it, love it and request it to die.

No armour is the way to rise again

The stories of communities, organizations and movements that have been able to live beyond the era of their founders tend to encompass some constant features: They usually welcomed reformers and have been able to tell new stories, alongside those of the founding era.

Reformers make space for a charisma that is foundational for the community to stay alive and fruitful, as well as to return to the original *charismatic questions*, changing the *answers* given to them. When the reformers do not appear, or are ostracized and not recognized, charismatic ideals and experiences inevitably wane due to a lack of grip on the present, and, consequently, to a radical shortage of young people and "vocations" brought about by the inability to revive the first message and the first experience. Its most involved and motivated members experience a deep moral and spiritual crisis: In a first stage, they suffer from a lack of young people and new vocations, then they become indifferent and, in the end, they even feel some joy, because their disappointment leads them not to wish on anyone their same sad existential experience. Therefore, this crisis manifests itself as a no good way of ageing, leading to read life as decadence and decline. When and if these symptoms emerge in the concrete charismatic communities, it is clear that there is an urgent need for reform.

At the stage of the foundation, charismas generate more seeds than just those that manage to flourish in the first season: There are some intended to sprout in the subsequent ones, when the first seeds will have become old. The full potential of a charisma is greater than what can be manifested in the times of foundation. There are deep veins that do not surface right away: Despite being connected to the same source they are meant to come to the fore during droughts or after earthquakes. The concrete forms of poverty, loved and embraced by the Church during her two millennia, have been much more than those loved and embraced by Jesus of Nazareth and his disciples. The poor of Mother Teresa, Francesca Cabrini, Don Oreste Benzi and Hans Frei are not those who lived in Pilate's Palestine: These new charismas have done "greater things" for poverty in the name of Jesus Christ than Jesus himself or his historical community. A similar process is repeated for each individual charisma, which in the course of its development uncovers dimensions that did not emerge during the historical life of founders. Founders create communities-movements through a *process of discovering* the charisma, which is revealed gradually, and throughout the community's entire existence. The more difficult part concerns realizing, in an already established community, that this progressive discovery of a charisma continues even after its first foundation, and when this process is stopped or interrupted, what becomes sterile is the first charisma.

Sometimes it is the historical Francis who understands that the church to rebuild is not the church of San Damiano; at other times, it is the living spirit of Francis, among the Franciscans, that understands and does it. It is a Francis after Francis to complete the foundation of Francis and Bernard. However, when the foundation process is stuck with the first generation because it is considered complete and final with the death of the founder, it prevents the charisma from thriving and being revealed to the full, as well as from illuminating and explaining the facts and events of the founding generation. Just as we do it at home when we place some apples among the kiwis to make them ripen. In a mysterious but real inter-temporal kind of solidarity, the Francis that lives on after himself equally serves the first Francis. We would know less of his charisma without Bonaventure or

Bernardino of Siena. The first beneficiaries with the courage of the reformers are the founders themselves since they can say new and sometimes different things thanks to those who freed them from the limitations of their historical time. Reformers make the rocks roll away from the "tombs" of their founders. They are "resurrected" from their graves. True reforms are not only the actualization of the charisma: They are a *continuation* of the first foundation, with different but no less wonderful fruits and miracles. The second "miracles" are essential for unlocking the first ones.

Once deemed so precious, why then are reforms rare and always very painful? The first charismatic groups, in order to survive in the time in which they were born (all societies have a tendency to kill the prophets that could save them) had to carry out a sort of *hybridization* between new and old, in order to prevent the old from rejecting and choking the new. So, around the first good shrubs, the first generation naturally develops an ancillary vegetation to protect new seedlings, which allows them to flourish in the shade of other, more robust and weatherproof plants. This way, charismatic intuitions are surrounded by an entire subsidiary bush; they are covered with infrastructure, languages, written and unwritten rules, sometimes self-produced and sometimes inherited from tradition or the specific historical context. At a certain point, this hybridization – which is a different process and one that is parallel to the *ideological* production that accompanies the development of an *ideal*, as we have addressed earlier – results in a *straitjacket*, which blocks growth and shuts down the future. Reforms come to slow down, and in the best scenarios, they break the initial coating which has gradually become a straitjacket, the protective shield that has turned into a rigid steel armour.

The most challenging aspect of this liberation effort dwells in the difficulty of recognizing the straitjacket of the "person" who wears it. In the biggest and richest charismatic communities, hybridization between old and new has been profound and lasted for many years, and so pieces of armour got into the flesh, and the skin has grown over parts of the armour. The first place that encloses the intermingling of old and new is the very rule written by founders and left to their heirs, where items of novelty and coating coexist, without the very founders being aware of it, or perhaps in a small part only.

Reforms, then, are painful because by removing the armour a few shreds of skin are also taken off. This is where the almost invincible trend comes from whereby communities reject the very reformers of whom they would have a vital need. The natural and necessary need to protect and save a charisma ends up curbing the attempts at reform. In the name of their own purity, charismas get condemned to sterility. Purity becomes unfruitful *purism*, for not having had enough charismatic courage to snatch a few flaps of skin, creating a wound through which the only salvation would have passed.

Every translation is also a betrayal, and the fear of betrayal should not prevent the success of the translation. Given that without translation, the beautiful poems of charismas are incomprehensible to those who would listen to them but speak and understand a different language.

There are many experiences and charismatic ideals that today would still be alive and/or fruitful if they had been able to generate a reform from the pain of a wound. Reforms succeed way too infrequently because the true reformers are suffocated or because false prophets are followed – or both – also because wise reformers and false prophets are very much alike, even too much. And the reformers that are too easy to spot are almost always false reformers. The first criterion for recognizing reformers is the fact that they do not present themselves as such to communities. We should always be wary of the reformers who attribute this title to themselves and introduce themselves as "reformers by vocation" to the people. The first art of reformers is to act as craftsmen: They collect the stones of yesterday, sometimes even the rubble, and with these they build a new San Damiano with humility and hope: It may be smaller than the old church, however, in its humble silence you can listen to the first voice, and sometimes learn to pray again.

When there's light again

The decisive experiences of life are not easy to recognize and call by name, because if we could understand their blissful nature, their injury would leave no mark (or sign) on us, they would not *mean (signify) or teach* anything to us.

If we were able to decipher the birth of a new purity along a pathway that opens up to us, and maybe its impurity; if we could understand that we are becoming stronger while a disease is making us experience the greatest weakness; if we could realize that we are actually creating a new and truer docility as we strive with all our strength to keep our business alive, these experiences would lose their value; the very grace/*charis* which has saved the world so far, and which continues to save us, would simply disappear. Like nature, like the smiles of children who convert us and give us the greatest joy because they do not want to either convert or make us happy, because they are simply so. Voluntarism is used in many things, but not in the really decisive matters, where we only need to learn to "know how to be" in unawareness.

When a person starts on a path of ideals following a vocation – whether religious, civil, artistic or poetic – at the beginning there is always the experience of a strong new light, amplified, often by the strength of youth. A light that is inside and outside at the same time, which turns on the best part in us: It calls to it, we recognize it as a good voice that we have always waited for, and so a journey following the voice begins. That is when we move all the furniture inside the room of our soul, because we want to shed the new light on the entire space. At the beginning of every vocation there is a voice and an emptied room that becomes very, very bright. It nourishes us, quenches our thirst, fills us and makes us feel alive. We do not want anything else, nor do we need anything else.

After this stage of naked light, which can last many years, a second stage begins. Day after day, we start resettling the room with new objects, furniture, ornaments, paintings, curtains, cupboards, clothes, statues and crucifixes. It is the building up of religion and worship. It could not be otherwise, because the symbolic construction of an illuminated environment from the original spiritual experience is the first act by which human beings recognize and love vocations. At first, this construction and this fulfilling are mostly social and collective: The furniture and cabinets are neither built nor bought by ourselves; instead, the community provides us with these elements. The only space that remains for us is for a photo of our parents or girlfriend. After some time, if the vocation grows well and thrives, gradually and almost always unconsciously, one feels the need to customize the furniture and start adding new items and personal things to the earlier furniture. This is a particularly creative moment of life, which usually coincides with the years of youthful maturity, when that first voice gradually takes the form of our personality, and a symbiosis between the light and the most beautiful part of our character is created. From "consumers" we start to become "producers" of light, in a sublime type of reciprocity game: We are conscious of not being the masters of the light that we consume and produce, but we feel that the work we are doing would not come to Earth without our part, without our industrious and creative "yes", the one that allowed that *logos*-voice to become "flesh". Poets know well that the voice that inspires them is not their property, but they also know that without their efforts, docility and talent, that voice would not become poetry, their poems.

The creations and creatures multiply along with success and the growing feeling of bearing much fruit into a thriving existence. Without us becoming aware of it during the process, the first inner room begins to lose brightness, because the new furniture and new products, added to the old ones, begin to fill all the space, to the point of blocking the window and overshadowing the light. However – and this is a central aspect in this filling process – the subjective experience made by those who blocked the window with their works is not the one of darkness. Born from the encounter with the first light, their works illuminate the environment with a light that is very similar to the original one, to the point of not being able to distinguish them clearly. This way the faint light that penetrates from the outside is replaced by the light that emanates from their works, until the latter takes it over entirely.

The light changes and decays every day, but our eyes will gradually get used to the decreasing and different kind of light. This is how we get used to the light of our works and of our fruits, even to the point of forgetting the colours of the room of our youth. But when the light of our home begins to come only from our illuminated works, creativity is reduced, the light loses its brightness, we do not get surprised by anything we do anymore. The process is slow and can also take many years before we and others realize that the light has been changed. This is a form of *spiritual narcissism* that often imprisons people – specifically those with strong vocations and great talents. They feed on themselves, thinking that they are still nourished by the first light – also because, in a sense, these two are (almost) the same thing. There are people who for the longest time stay in their stuffed room which is illuminated only by reflected light, which is increasingly more artificial and dimmer, deriving from their own constructs.

One day, the reflected and artificial light is extinguished because of a lack of feed. And here there are three possible scenarios. The first is adapting to living in this darkness: The pupils enlarge until they manage to see in almost total darkness. To survive, the other senses are developed, so sight is lost without realizing it. Some people, however, when their room is left with no more light feel an uncontrollable desire to quit: They escape and look for another home, they return to their previous existence, to the meeting of their vocation, and no longer want to know about the light that has seduced them and now is but deception and condemnation for them.

But there may be a third outcome: *Reform*, and the beginning of a new spiritual life. Having touched bottom with the extinguishing of the light, a dream comes to save us: One night we dream of the first light in all its colours again and wake up with an invincible longing for real sunshine (many people who become blind continue to see colours in their dreams for years). And once awake, we frantically begin to remove objects, artefacts, furniture, which now appear to us dull and heavy, to free the window and see the original coloured light again. And so, as we are thirsty for sunshine, we start a new process of liberation from the room of artefacts, and from many idols that had accumulated over the years of worship.

But it is here that another surprise awaits us. When, at the end of the clearing, the room is empty again and we finally reach the window, we open it and realize that outside it is the time of night. Where did the first light that we all longed for end up? To the years that passed between the first light and the reform, instances of human pain, limited experiences, suffering, injustice, death, mistakes and sins (especially natural idolatry) got inserted. And we do not find that sun anymore. At this point, some people are convinced that the sun is gone forever, and the spiritual path is blocked; others leave home, begin to walk the Earth, and are waiting for a new dawn. There begins a new stage of spiritual and moral life, which is among the rarest, highest and most extraordinary ones. You find yourself in an empty room and, having been liberated, looking out towards a sky that does not light up. Reform is the work done to free us from darkness to get us to another darkness. With a crucial novelty, however, the new dark is true, airy, spacious and alive. The main effort of spiritual life is learning to distinguish the second darkness from the first one, because they are very different. The first imprisons, the second saves us.

After reforms, both on a personal and community level, we must learn to *see* in this darkness. That is why only a few succeed, and most people get stranded in the first post-reform season, because of the disappointment over not finding the light they long for (communities do not like and tend to "kill" authentic reformers as they expected light from them and found darkness, and it happens all too often that they love false prophets who are great builders of new artificial lighting systems).

Reforms, those of the soul but also of communities, are successful if they manage to *stay* in this new darkness, if they learn to live in it, to love it, and then to stretch their eyes until they see the stars in the depth of the dark sky, and discover their new and different light, "*clarite et pretiose et belle*" (clear and precious and beautiful). Even the night has its own brightness: Farmers and nocturnal wayfarers are well aware of this. It is a less intense but more real light than the one coming from the streetlamps.

The first result of any reform is taking notice that the light of adult life is different from the artificial one that we had built, it is less dazzling than the one instilled in youth, but it is no less true. It is the splendour of the light of this truth that makes us walk the long nights of reforms, those of the soul and those of the community. It is in this waiting that, gently and lovingly, the sentinels announce the dawn to us.

The illness of light is deadly

The processes of change in VBOs are particularly complex and delicate because, unlike in many economic or bureaucratic organizations where change is planned and guided towards the objectives set by the owners, in ideal-based organizations reform is actually a march into the unknown.

When the self-styled reformer is a false prophet, he presents himself as the bearer of certainty about change, as someone who knows what the good is that awaits the community at the end of the path advocated, wanted and promoted by him. Like an angel who is *the bearer of only and all light*.

One of the elements that make it complex and difficult to overcome the moments of crisis in ideal-driven and charismatic communities is the appearance of false reformers. As a matter of fact, if the community is not alive anymore, to the point of not even feeling the need for reform, neither good nor bad "prophets" are born into it. If the community is alive, the good and the bad prophets tend to appear *simultaneously*, and the more lively and fruitful the original charisma still is, the more prophets emerge. The abundance of false prophets is also a way to reveal the charismatic vitality of a community. And the more light there is in the charisma, the more frequent, subtle and dangerous Gnostic heresies are. The early churches were full of apostles *and* false prophets. Therefore, we must not make the mistake of thinking that positive stages only produce good prophets and those of crisis only bad ones, because historical reality shows the exact opposite to be the case. After all, it was the same spiritual fertility of early Christianity to generate Paul of Tarsus and Simon Magus.

The historical and concrete forms assumed by false prophecies are many. In ideal-driven and/or charismatic communities, the most subtle and pernicious false prophecies and false reforms are those that have recourse to the register of *light*. They are variations on and updates of the ancient *Gnostic* heresy because they present themselves as an offer of new light and different knowledge. Gnosticism, in its rich and varied expressions, was the main ideological enemy of the Christianity of the first centuries. Penetrated in many communities, it could have decreed the death of Christianity if it had not been fought hard and eventually defeated thanks to the action of the best prophets and theologians – from Irenaeus to Augustine.

Spiritual and ideal-connected experiences are naturally and radically exposed to Gnostic seduction, because of them being essentially experiences of light and intelligence. Those who follow an ideal or a charisma are attracted by the new light and the different words (*logos*).

They discover the gift of new eyes that show new horizons, new heaven, new beauties, and with a bright intelligence that opens a different understanding of the world and things.

It should not be surprising, therefore, that in these communities the Gnostic stage arrives readily. It threatens especially those with the brightest and most spiritual charismas, because it is also an illness which can develop as a form of neurosis: Their most brilliant part gets ill. Spiritual experiences remain authentic and generate good life until they keep their connection with history, while they remain incarnate and therefore limited experiences, partial and intertwined with darkness as long as the spirit remains in the flesh and the one follows the laws and the rhythms of the other. Many charismatic experiences are lost upon their birth because the spirit becomes disembodied and evaporates in search of perfection without any shade. For these reasons, Gnostic stages also accompany the historical existence of the founders, and if communities survive beyond the life of their founders, it is because these temptations have not had the upper hand – many communities born from genuine charismas were spent after a few years because their founders were eventually seduced and devoured by Gnostic neurosis.

But it is in the stage right after foundation that the Gnostic temptation becomes almost obligatory and always decisive. Facing the end of the era of true "miracles" and "resurrections" that had been the normal way of life of the community's founding stage, some people start to think they can recreate the early wonders with certain techniques and spiritual drugs. They do like athletes who, no longer able to repeat their first record, instead of changing their training and working hard, they fall into the trap of doping. Gnosticism is a form of spiritual doping which promises the performance of youth without work and effort, and if it is not decisively countered, it infects the whole community very quickly.

It is, thus, on this suffering and frustration over not being able to repeat the first charismatic performance, on the unconquerable nostalgia for the signs and the climate of earlier times where the Gnostic plant easily takes root. Instead of starting from the core of the first message, necessarily made of flesh and spirit, the Gnostic reformer performs a twofold task: Reconstructing a partial and disembodied image of the original charisma and adding secret revelations that – he says – he has come into possession through private experiences or special communications, and which are adorned by the spectacular and pseudo-mystic elements and techniques that supposedly allow for a deeper access to the ideal and spiritual message. The Gnostic type of reform is therefore accompanied by the promise of special mystical experiences that are accessible only to those few who have been introduced to the secrets and mysteries, around which it establishes a messianic power and its main promise. These are always elitist, non-transparent experiences that are neither popular nor on the side of the poor. The devaluation of concrete experience and the body then creates almost inevitably an ethical *exception*, which allows for enlightened carnal acts and actions that are harmful to others, but legitimate and necessary for the inhabitants of this new "colour" kingdom.

They are Baroque constructs, they are colourful worlds populated by many fantastic beings and "truths" that do not appear in the first, original message. And the followers of these false prophets soon take the looks and attitudes of the initiated; they undergo an aesthetic change also in the expression of their eyes and facial features and separate from the not (yet) illuminated people as the new "saints".

When a charisma is alive and healthy, it is very easy to identify false prophets who are moved by personal material interests or are intent schismatics; however, *the false prophets of light and intelligence* are much more difficult to recognize and call by name, because they use the same symbolic repertoire and the same words that had founded the community one day and attracted many people to it. They are devouring wolves disguised as meek lambs, and sometimes as the good shepherd. The severe crises of ideal-driven communities are always *crises of light and intelligence*. For this reason, the choice of heresies of light and intelligence is particularly abundant, especially and exactly *during the most serious crises*. And for the same reason, many times false prophets are not recognized, they are successful, and they kill communities.

A fundamental job to manage deep crises and major reforms is, therefore, being able to recognize the Gnostic symptoms from the very moment they appear as renewal and salvation. It is a rather difficult job, because the Gnostic reformer, unlike other false prophets, uses truths and words that are actually present in the original, genuine charisma, and builds his or her speech up using parts and phrases from the speeches of the founder. From the beginning, *the intelligence of the snake* has manifested itself in history in words and discourses similar to and more seductive than those of Elohim. The Gnostic chromosomes are in the DNA of the genuine charisma because the gnosis builds salvation combining some foundational elements of the genome in a different way. It deletes the ordinary, normal or grey ones, as well as the mestizos, and reassembles only the brightest part of the original genetic material, creating a body that has all the features present in the first body. Hence, the Gnostic reform appears tremendously charming and bright: As the elixir of eternal youth, as the tree of life, like a picture of us when we were 20 years old that magically takes life.

The Gnostic reform proposals are therefore presented as days where it is always sunshine, and in the name of this light without shadow they refuse the dark dimension, which is only so because it is true, and due to limits. Incarnation, imperfection and sin become cursed words, condemned as a scandal to be overcome, in order to create the new era of full maturity, which is about to begin. This is the proposal of an *eschaton* in reverse: While the authentic spiritual experiences live an imperfect *already* and point to a *not yet*, which is never fully reached, the gnosis will present itself as a perfected *already*, the completion of an imperfect *already have*. Gnostic reformers are always brighter than the founders because they lack the shadow of true reality. Only the body can cast a shadow when it gets in contact with sunlight.

In these false reforms, death is absent from the scene of their fake passions. They are "gospels" without the Calvary and the cross, the stone does not roll, and the tomb is just a comfortable bedroom. These are very bad takes on the mourning of life. They reject life in order not to get their feet dirty on the only pathway possible for humans under the sun. Resurrections without crucifixes do not save anyone. They are ghosts that drift apart from the wounded flesh of others and from the victims, and imprison people inside cages of psychic and emotional consumerism. Gnostic false prophets are revealed by the absence of the marks of the nails on their bodies and the bodies of those that they touch and embrace.

The risk of generating freedom

A particularly important phenomenon is the so-called "mission shift", which occurs when the organizations, movements and associations become something different during their development and move away from the purpose that had generated them, because some activities that were born to serve the mission at the beginning end up becoming the *order* instead of the *means*.

Ancillary activities start to seize opportunities, or it happens because of some need, and then gradually, and almost always unintentionally, these activities absorb increasingly more energy, as well as the resources that once were used to develop the original mission. This falls within many important phenomena where the line between the good, the less good and the bad is almost impossible to detect, because they live inside one another, they grow together, and when the "evil" becomes clear and visible, it is almost always too late to intervene effectively. Organizations and people change together. The original identity remains alive and fertile until it is able to co-evolve with people but as soon as an invisible, but very real, "critical point" is passed, the fruit of change ends up poisoning identity. In this paradox lies a lot of the quality and outcomes of the organizational evolution processes.

A change of the mission and the tension between the means and ends are important facts in any form of organized life, but they are crucial in those organizations arising from ideals, charismas or great and complex "missions". Here a change of mission is not only a delicate process, but it can also lead to their death.

These communities and movements may also die when transforming into something too different from the original charisma – and sometimes they are already dead although they appear to be in great health. A school founded by an educational charisma can die because it closes, but it can also die in terms of its charisma, since it has gradually become an institution that has lost touch with its original mission. It will still bring fruit, but those are fruits of a different flavour, even if the community cannot notice this change that it creates and on which it feeds because its palate has gradually adapted to it. And so, after being established to promote a cause or serve an ideal, it suddenly finds itself promoting and serving another one or other ones. The servant becomes the master.

If an enterprise of footwear was founded yesterday only as a means to make profits (a very rare occurrence), its nature does not change substantially if you move first to the bags industry, then on to sport and ultimately to the financial-speculative sector. Just as it frequently happens that an ancillary type of activity (for example, products for shoes) gradually becomes the main activity. In all these cases, the mission (making profits) remains consistent, only the ways and means to embody it change.

Things are radically different when we are not dealing with a company but a missionary religious order that founded a hospital to serve the poor and proclaim the Gospel a hundred years ago. In this case, we cannot stay easy if over time the hospital has become increasingly large and efficient, and so it has drained a growing number of economic, spiritual and human resources, and the Gospel and the poor have been gradually distanced from its horizon. Until one day they disappear altogether, when the hospital becomes so beautiful and expensive that it will only treat wealthy customers – it is a shame though that in order to grow and become so big, it has consumed almost all the energy of the community. Here the transmutation of the means into ends may simply lead to the death of the original mission, because day after day the work-child has eaten up its parent.

This process is particularly difficult to manage because these different organizations live and grow with a *radical uncertainty* about their future, which opens up and is revealed to them only as tomorrow becomes today. When work is started or a community is opened in a new country, nobody knows where the new foundation will lead, because in ideal-driven and charismatic organizations the main indigence is not knowing the arrival point of the journey.

The only knowledge that is given concerns its origin, and even this is imperfect and partial. They are like those ancient messengers, who had the message to be transmitted written on the back of their head. The real name of the communities born of charismas is revealed only when there is someone who reads it and explains it. The recipient of the message is not the community that carries and transmits it. The discovery of each identity is never a narcissistic process, but it is a gift we receive from those who can look at us differently. And charisma is never given for the sole consumption of the community which embodies it. When we no longer feel the need for somebody other than us to read the message that we bring written on the back of our head, and we try to interpret ourselves alone by looking at mirrors, charismas become minimal chores, socially irrelevant, if not harmful, and will wane soon.

So when a new work is born from a community we cannot know if the "baby" will be the realization of the promise or the one who will kill us one day, despite unwillingness to do so or unawareness, whether it will be Isaac or Oedipus. We cannot know their fate until it is fulfilled in the unfolding ambivalences, contradictions, in the meetings at the crossroads of history. At other times, though, it is not the works and activities that distort the ideal-driven communities and make them die. In some cases, it is the *community itself*, born of a charisma, that ends up killing it.

False reformers, missed or delayed reforms, can cause a crisis which is so radical and devastating it may actually overcome the community itself. Here the generations that follow the one of the foundation cannot preserve the charisma and make it grow: The founder produces children who end up killing the charisma that they have inherited.

The greatest fear of those who found an ideal-driven community or organization is that the next generation, their "children", go astray, and betray the charismatic identity. This fear is in the chromosomes of each good foundation, and its absence simply reveals that we are not dealing with a charisma but with an ordinary organization. But this founder knows, or should know, that the truly deadly mistake is to transform this natural fear into phobia or panic, and so hinder and prevent the continuation of the original experience.

Exposure to the distortion of the mission and the original charisma is the precondition for its fulfilment, its fecundity and its good growth. In the foundation of an ideal or charismatic organization, the time when the founders pass through this specific and decisive test arrives promptly. The possibility of continuing the charismatic experience beyond the founder, and then the transition of the charisma from one generation to another are almost all in the capacity to manage this vital, inevitable and decisive tension. The temptation has to be overcome and the generation that will come after the founder should be put in a position to be born, live and grow for real. In every child *there may be Oedipus hiding*, in every child *there hides Oedipus*. In every child *there may be Isaac hiding*, in every child *there hides Isaac*.

The latest and greatest temptation of all charismatic foundations is to prevent the "child" from being born out of fear that he or she may kill his or her father. The charisma is totally identified by the founder with his own person, who is blinded and makes it non-transmissible, thereby preventing it from a rebirth many times in many generations. And so the charisma dies with the founder. Many communities have died simply because of this, for *lack of generosity* which is what *prevents them from real generation*. The greater the foundational charisma, the stronger the temptation is not to generate for fear of dying. No foundation of a community can escape the risk of its degeneration, because if it does, it surely will degenerate: If it evolves, it can get lost along the way, but if it prevents evolution, it will get lost for sure.

Communities are generated and regenerated when those who have founded or re-founded them are able to "give birth" to men and women who become free to the point of giving their lives for the same "mission" of the founders. In this freedom there hides the possibility of abusing, perverting, injuring and even killing the gift. Without this radically risky and vulnerable gift of freedom the charismas do not bloom over time, they wither for lack of children, or because the children generated and brought up without this freedom become too "little" to be able to repeat the miracles of the first generation. Only risky and vulnerable confidence is capable of the generativity necessary for the charismas to continue to flourish.

The wonderful mystery of transmitting gifts between generations lives in the space opened by the vital tension between trust and betrayal. Our children can become better than we are, if we also give them the freedom to become worse than us, and to betray our dreams and our promises. Perhaps there is no greater gift than this.

The traps of "we"

The biggest challenge in all community experience is being able to create a "we" that does not end up devouring the "I" of the individuals who have created it. Collective nouns are good and on the side of life only if they are accompanied and preceded by names and personal pronouns. The "we" without the "I" is the origin of all community pathologies and illiberal regimes, even when they arise as a promise of liberation and are clothed with the robes of salvation.

Communities can only serve their people if they recognize that they are *second*, allowing the first person singular to precede the plural. When this natural order of plurals and the singulars is reversed or denied, personal paths fail, vocations wither, the community betrays itself.

The destiny of every vocation is the generation of new life, the liberation of slaves from the pharaohs, beyond the sea. But every vocation is also a great love story. Its good development over time, therefore, lies in the concrete possibility of being able to hold together the call to the liberation of the oppressed and the delicate management of narcissistic emotions present in every love affair. In the beginning there is *eros*. The voice comes to us, it calls us and seduces us, and we find ourselves in the dream of dreams. All around us bursts out singing and is illuminated by a new sun inside, which is truer and brighter than the one shining outside. All the feelings light up, the heart moves and is moved, we feel and touch the voice that calls us like bread, like people. It is a sublime experience and essential to start each high flight under the sun. And those who have got to know it keep looking for it all their life. But in order for the vocation to continue its good development, the maturation of eros into *philia* (friendship) is needed. When that happens, the first call becomes an experience of company and fraternity. We exit the central and the prevailing register of emotions and passion and we start building communities. The feelings and the falling in love do not necessarily disappear, but they are neither the only nor the first language anymore. This is a very nice period of life and it is generally very long: This is when the vocation builds new cities, it carries out works and an experience of a new kind of fertility and new children takes place. To Ishmael, the son of the flesh, Isaac, the son of promise is added. Faith also changes, and from an emotional and intimate experience it becomes a great history of a people, blooming in the community. The same first love is discovered in the love of the others, and a new alliance is celebrated together. The vocation opens up and it becomes a collective event. *Eros* stays alive even in the age of the *philia* because every form of love is co-essential if we want to live it well: There is no good *philia* (or authentic *agape*) without *eros*. But its maturation into *philia* changes *eros* forever, it opens and humanizes it.

In vocations that do not fail along the way, *philia*, arising from the maturation of *eros*, blooms in turn into *agape*. This is the time of full maturity when the flowers of spring become the fruits of summer. The community that has kept the first vocation and turned it into a shared and fruitful collective adventure now becomes the springboard towards new spiritual horizons. The community does its job of a good pedagogue and finally introduces the person into adulthood. We continue to live with and for other fellow travellers, but with an all-new sense of freedom and truth. Here the liberation promised by the first call reaches a first milestone: One is freed from the very community that had been donated to us. We understand that we have been sent to a larger community of our own: That of all. It turns out that the family that welcomed us was not the last word, but only the penultimate one, that our destiny is in the land of all, that the sky above the home garden is too small to hold our call to infinity. And we take off, even when we stay in the same house. There is no truer or more radical freedom than the one gushing from agape, when it really becomes *anima mundi* and we get to know gratuitousness. Those who come across these agapic souls feel the heartbeat of the whole universe, no longer limited by the boundaries of a community or a specific charisma. Their identities become radically universal; their communities always have the door open.

Not all vocations manage to reach their *agape* stage. Many, too many, are stuck in the previous stages. The most common outcome is stopping at the "erotic" phase. People remain within the register of feelings, emotions and romance for life. Those who never leave the first dream fall into this vocational narcissism, and they reinvent and recreate it when it disappears. Instead of reading the end of the stage as a sign and an invitation to evolve into a different, more mature love, they remain entangled in the toils of their own feelings, in a constant search for emotionally exciting narcissistic "spiritual" experiences, capable of stimulating the senses and passions. Life becomes a continuous flying from flower to flower in search of new, fresh and intoxicating pollen. They keep looking for friendships, meetings and new communities, "consumed" and left after a very short time, as soon as nourishment is finished. Life becomes a unique, monotonous and repetitive experience of "emotional" consumption, without ever moving on to the "production" stage and the liberation of the slaves.

Emotions and feelings are only the dawn and not the sunny midday of a vocation. The first exclusive and satiating dialogue must become a dialogue with the people in time, a dialogue with the poor, the slaves, with all the voices of the world, with that of the birds, the sea and the stones. One voice is not enough today to express that first voice that called us yesterday. Too many people lose faith in the truth of the voice of the first meeting because they seek it in the wrong places, in the infancy of vocation, in the feelings and passions of the heart. That was only the cradle, but when you are grown up cots must serve the children, ours and those of others. Biblical faith is never individual consumption: It is always the generation of salvations not yet accomplished, for others, and sometimes for ourselves. Noah went on the ark of salvation that he had built by vocation. Moses, on the other hand, did not reach the promised land; he saw it only from a distance. When we receive a call, we do not know if we are to save ourselves, too, or only others. But what really matters is to keep walking, until the very end Mount Nebo can be a good place to die if before we have seen our people reach salvation.

Usually, these blocked vocations arrive in times of great crises, when the natural habituation to emotions boils down to cancel the ability to experience pleasure from emotional consumption. An absolute dryness of feeling settles in, which is confused with spiritual aridity, and having identified the vocation with that first and only nourishment, people feel lost. Sometimes this great drought can open a new phase and mark the beginning of spiritual life. But this happy event is rare, because those who are in these "erotic" arid phases, instead of being helped to make a radical change of register, are very often encouraged to continue their inner consumption to regain the lost emotions. And the disease becomes incurable. They do not understand that in order to move from one stage of life to another they only need to learn *to die*.

No less common is the block at the stage of *philia*, which is harder to spot as illness and vocational failure, because the line between *philia* and *agape* is far more blurred than the one between *eros* and *philia*. Persons who reach the stage of *philia* experience fruits that resemble the ones typical of *agape*. When, leaving the individual eros behind, the chorus of community life is reached is we live a new kind of fertility, especially when compared with the sterility of an erotic phase prolonged beyond its natural span. This is why it is easy to be trapped in the community *philia*, and not to arrive ever to the true *agape* phase. When we reach the age of *philia*, our individual identity ends up coinciding with the community identity almost inevitably. We identify with it to the point of not being able to say "I" but only "we". The arrival of the agape stage then becomes a liberation from community *philia*, a great blessing which comes as a wound that can be very deep and painful. We cannot pass the age of eros and enter that of agape without crossing *philia*, because the agape communities are the resurrection of the *philia* communities, and hence they are essential. When, in fact, personal identity has completely identified with a given group for years, to move to the new freedom of *agape* we go through a real death. The *philia* community must disappear to make way for the *agape* community. This disappearance brings with it all: The charisma, our personality, not infrequently even faith. This loss is total and radical, but there is no other way to reach the land of *agape*. The wisdom of those who accompany people during the crisis of philia is knowing how to indicate the promised land beyond the waves sweeping away everything, knowing to show a tree beyond the sea that is a lot more fruitful and lush than the dying bonsai.

Only those who have already passed the stage of *philia* (and that of *eros*) should accompany those who are still struggling in the ford. Too many rivers Jordan are never crossed because they have never been shown by the guides or were confused with the River Nile of ancient slavery.

Note

1 On an Introduction to the economics of these organizations, see Bruni and Smerilli (2015) and Antoci, Bruni, Russo and Smerilli (2020).

2 Narrative capitals

Reviving the tree of ideals

The narrative capital is the *first mechanism for selecting* new members of the organization or community. We love many things, but above all we love wonderful stories, those that awaken the deepest and truest part of our soul, that make us become better simply by listening to them. The greater our ideals and our soul is, the greater the promise contained in the narrative capital must be in order to activate and make us become part of that same story. Small stories attract people with small desires and ideals; great stories conquer great souls; extraordinary stories attract extraordinary people.

In the early days of its foundation, this narrative capital is the only asset that a community possesses, especially those movement-communities that arise from spiritual ideals – inside and outside religions. We nourish ourselves with the life that is generated, with the first stories and "miracles", with life and the words of the founders that are still lived and told to each other. The new life is immediately a gospel, *fresh good news*. Those who are reached by that generative story recognize their own story, past and future in it. In those early days, the rate of accumulating the narrative capital is very high, and its growth is exponential. Most of this special heritage is formed during the very first few years, sometimes in the early months or days. Its "productivity" is extraordinary and astonishing: In any environment it is enough to evoke those first stories to witness authentic miracles that are as and (sometimes) more impressive than the first ones. Saying and repeating the phrases and facts of the beginning produce literally extraordinary effects, which, in addition to making the community grow, also fuels the conviction of the truth and strength of the announced ideal in those who announce it, in a very powerful and admirable virtuous circle (identifying stories – announcing them – bearing fruits – strengthening ideals – announcing them again).

If the "charisma" at the origin of these experiences is rich and innovative, and the founder is generous and creative, one can feed on the stories and words of the early days for decades – even for centuries – without feeling the need to add a single new one. But it is within this richness that the so-called *parasitic syndrome* develops. Almost inevitably and always *unintentionally*, the immense fruits that the stories of the past generate become an obstacle to the creation of new narrative capital. And today we begin to live with the income of yesterday – like the entrepreneur who stops innovating and generating new income because he lives very well on the revenues of past capitals. The bigger the first narrative capital, the longer the stage of life fuelled by the revenue is. This is a form of the so-called "paradox of abundance" (or "resource curse"), the trap in which rich countries fall thanks to a single natural resource, ending up impoverishing themselves precisely because of that enormous wealth. A spiritually rich founder and charisma can shift from "blessing" into "curse" without wanting or being aware of it, if the spiritual richness of their charisma makes it easier and faster to trigger a parasitic syndrome (which can already begin during the life of the founders themselves who stop innovating and nourish themselves above all from their past). Because, paradoxically, the greater the spiritual richness, the more likely it is that the parasitic syndrome is activated. Communities with simple founders and charismas have other problems, but they do not know the parasitic syndrome, which is a typical *disease of wealth*.

But unlike financial or real estate capitals, which can allow a constant or increasing flow of revenue, narrative capitals begin to age and shrink if they are not updated and renewed. For them, Edgar Morin's phrase is especially true: Everything that is not regenerating is degenerating. This obsolescence/degeneration can be extremely and dramatically rapid in times of acceleration of history (as ours is). From one day to the next, one finds oneself in a serious famine of stories to tell. Those first stories that were convincing and of a conversional power until yesterday, the ones that were our great treasure, had enchanted us and founded our individual and collective life become silent, cold, dead. The distance between the language and the challenges of the present and the stories of the past becomes enormous – here, again, the watchmen are young people: They are the first to report illness.

In ideal connected and charismatic histories, the *first stories* continue to speak in the second and future generations only if accompanied by the *second and third stories*. Franciscans have kept Franciscanism and Christianity alive by adding the stories of Francis to those of the Gospels, and Franciscans today keep Francis (and the Gospel) alive by adding their "acts" to those of the *Poverello of Assisi*. The first patrimony, the fathers' narrative gift, is not enough to keep on living: The gift of *children* is also indispensable – which is also a gift for fathers who manage to never die.

The exhaustion of narrative capital is the most common cause of the crisis and death of a values-based organization (VBO). It is not easy to escape from this deadly syndrome. Often one gets ill and suffers without even being able to get to the diagnosis, and the crisis is attributed to other causes (the lack of radical thought in young people, the evilness of the world, etc.). At other times we understand that the crisis has to do with our inability to narrate the heart of the charisma, we see that the narrative capital doesn't speak (to us) more, or doesn't speak enough, or speaks to the wrong people, but the wrong cure is chosen.

The most common bad cure is adding new stories that are easier to understand in the "present century", but that no longer have the DNA of the first story. It is only in the end that many understand that it's because we are simply telling another story. Thus, it happens that a community born of a charisma that wanted to evangelize the world of family, faced with the difficulty of continuing to explain the evangelical words of the first generation to themselves and their world, begins to deal with family policies, adoptions and natural methods after a time. These new stories are much closer to the changed cultural sensibility, much easier to explain and understand, more suitable for financing and finding advocates. But the decisive problem hiding in such steps – that are common today – concerns the *narrative capital* directly. The new association can no longer use the first narrative capital, which remains a resource for the archives or for a phrase to quote on Christmas cards. Here there is no *grafting* of new stories on the old tree, but only *replacement* of the first narrative capital with the new one. In some cases, which are a *species* of this *genus*, there is a first phase when the new part of the narrative capital tries to maintain contact with its original component. But the new and more successful stories gradually erode the old ones, until they are consumed entirely.

For many people, these transformations and evolutions are inherent in the nature of things and history – they have always been, and always will be there. Others see it as a serious and decisive problem. The new narrative capital, simple and easily understandable, does not attract *vocations*. The first generation had been able to conquer people who are willing to dedicate their lives to that ideal because they were fascinated by the prophecy and the radical nature of the promise. If the great difficulty of explaining the first message generates words that are simpler and simpler to understand because they are bereaved of their ideal charge, what happens is a change in the *type of people* attracted by that message. The person in the first generation who had made that ideal *the* or *an* identity dimension of their life (this is the essence of every vocation) gradually disappears and new members arrive in their place with an increasingly lighter adhesion. In other words, the new narrative capital no longer selects *vocations* but *sympathizers*, or workers employed in works (life should be spent on God or on a world without poverty, not on "corporate social responsibility").

This is how thousands of charismatic communities and spiritual movements born in the twentieth century and in past centuries are becoming extinct. Sometimes, new institutions are born from their death, at other times they die and that is all, when faced with the probable distortion of identity the community and its leaders react by hindering or preventing any updating of the first narrative capital. They continue to tell the first stories, with the same language, with the same words that no longer fascinate anyone.

A third, equally unhappy, outcome is the re-absorption of the charisma within the tradition that the same charisma would have wanted to innovate and change. Faced with the difficulty of explaining – to oneself and to others – the charismatic importance of one's own community, one renounces to the specific and new components, and "returns" to do the same traditional activities that one wanted to innovate – at a young age, people want to announce the good news to other religions and non-believers, as adults, however, they go back to do catechism for confirmation.

These and many more are the scenarios that we will explore in depth later on. We will try to understand what good paths of the future exist whereby ideals can continue to nourish the consciousness of the world, so that the grafting of new stories on the first functions generates a new bloom, new fruits and new colours. We will ask ourselves: Is it really possible to update and regenerate the narrative capitals of our communities? Or is their dying inevitable? What are the generative transformations? How do we understand whether we are betraying the promise or fulfilling it? These are challenging and tricky questions and answers, but above all, they are necessary ones.

Avoiding false resurrections

The most tenacious and constant search that humans conduct on Earth is the search for *consolation*. It is impossible to give it up, especially in difficult times of existence, when the pain of the present and the uncertainty of the future generate the invincible temptation to construct illusions, in order not to die. Many people, even the great, interrupt their ethical and spiritual journey and regress when and because they give in to these terrible temptations.

Organizations, especially VBOs, are also deeply tempted by the cultivation of consolations. Often, faced with the urgency of having to change their course with courage and strength, they linger in the status quo full and satisfied and consoled by some fruit that continues to arrive. It is a serious and common mistake, which arises from confusing the "interests" of the narrative capital of yesterday with the wage of today's work – and so they live off the (decreasing) gains of the past believing, falsely, to live off of the new gains.

The destiny of every human community lies at the crossroads between the memory of the past, the management of the present and faith in the future. Roots, for example, are not the past of the plant. They are, *at the same time*, its memory, its life today and its blooming tomorrow. If, however, the roots are interpreted only as past, the typical illnesses of nostalgia inevitably arise, the first visible effect of which is the separation and distancing from the youth and from the reality of the present – young people flee away when they meet nostalgic communities with their eyes turned towards their origin. The only nostalgia generating a good present is that of the future. When the roots are read as the past, the narrative capital of the origin is transformed into a *mummy*, almost unavoidably. When the community (in rare cases) becomes aware of the ageing of the first stories and their imminent death, first the evolution of the mummified "corpse" is prepared, originated by the desire to save all that can be saved of the old body (the forms, the gaze, the features). What is left to the children is a corpse. The mummy does nothing but *eternalize* the death of the historical body. So it is the opposite of resurrection.

But resurrections are very rare events. Real death should be embraced; collective awareness should thrive as regards that first body which – notwithstanding its beauty and infinite charm – will never be there again. It should be accepted that the new life stories will be those of the future, which will also make people understand and "remember" the past. These authentic spiritual endeavours are proportionately as difficult as the first narrative capital was great and extraordinary, as the first historical body was "beautiful" – and so everybody wants to preserve it and not let it die.

But every "gospel" can only be written starting from a resurrection. Without the resurrection of Christ, his disciples would not have written anything, or would have written some Gnostic text that would have been added to the many generated in those early centuries of the late Roman Empire (and in all times of deep crisis, like ours). And so the narrative capital of parables, passion and death *would not be remembered in spirit*. And we would not have the prodigal son, the good Samaritan; we would not know of that crazy cry, nor of the other words resurrected on the first day after Saturday.

The *first* narrative capitals of the communities that are still alive and able to generate are the stories of the resurrection, because it is from these that the *second* stories of the more ancient historical facts are born. Stories that generate a lot of life for a long time are *not* those written by reporters *while* the events take place. Those chronicles die together with their characters. Unlike those accounts that are written by the "remnant" of the faithful who knew how to remain under the crosses, under the rubble of the temple, in the exiles, and who then recounted those facts of yesterday illuminated by life that had continued thanks to their tenacious fidelity. Even when the stories written after the events coincide with the stories written before, they are never the same, because the risen body is not the historical body. And instead, the most common error (because it is almost necessary) of the charismatic and ideal-driven communities is to think that narrative capital is an accomplished historical fact, the *ipsissima verba* of the founders. They do not *really* let them die, and therefore they do not allow them to be able, sometimes, to *really* rise again. Mummies cannot rise again. They are death and that is all – like Alessandro Manzoni's Donna Prassede, "when she says she was dead, everything is said" (*Promessi sposi*).

Narrative capitals are capable of a future if they are interpreted as a seed, and therefore as something alive and that, because it is a living thing, must die, and will only bring much fruit by dying, because that first seed will generate another hundred, a thousand. A seed lives, grows and dies precisely because it is alive – living things are alive *because* they are mortal. If instead the narrative capital of a charisma is read as a casket containing family jewellery, so shimmering and precious but dead, it is prevented from growing up, dying and bearing fruit. But how can we learn to rise again? No one can teach us. We can, however, at least avoid false resurrections. Just like in the Bible where the most bitter enemies of prophets are false prophets, in ideal-driven communities the mortal enemies of resurrections are false resurrections. The biblical prophets allowed for authentic resurrections of the people because they had, by their vocation, the infinite power to say that a first story was over. They made a second life possible after the deportation and destruction, because they did not deny the end – as the false prophets systematically did. Accepting *real* death did not prevent *real* resurrection. The inventors of fake resurrections (which are always forms of false prophecy) prevent the true resurrections because they continue to repeat that the "corpse" has not really died, that it is only an illusory death, sooner or later it will awaken. And so they propose and invent resuscitation techniques, build new defibrillators and convince the confused community to invest its last resources in attempting this "resurrection", which does not happen. It will not happen because it cannot happen – but the ideological force of this false prophecy manages to justify even failure, to the very end.

Another false resurrection is to hide the corpse. The disciples in Jerusalem, Emmaus and Galilee made it possible for the "miracle" of the resurrection to be fulfilled also because they did not conceal the corpse, which is the most common way of false resurrection. But the corpses only tell stories of death, and living things need living things in order to continue to live. Sometimes, paradoxically, "the concealment of the body" is unknowingly favoured by the founders and by those who had been most enchanted by the first narrative capital. It happens when founders and the first generation try to reassure themselves and make sure that their charisma and community will have a future. They write very detailed and closed rules, so that the first narrative capital does not die. Instead of believing and trusting their "children" and "grandchildren" who will have their own charismatic chromosomes, an insurance contract is stipulated with the future, and they are told: "You should not change the past". And so the healthy concern to save one's ideals produces the inevitable ageing of narrative capital, and the end of the experience. By preventing it from dying, they prevent it from rising again. In these cases, which are very deep traps, to save oneself there is a need for "children" and "grandchildren" – and sometimes "brothers and sisters" – capable of loving the fathers while also going against the letter of their fatherly recommendations, although knowing that they had been dictated by love and in good faith. Every "contract with the future" is a new concealment of the corpse, because such a pact is, as a matter of fact, the order to "start work" for the realization of one's own mummy.

Perhaps the early Church experienced something similar. We can imagine the historical phrases of Jesus that Peter and other disciples would have reminded Paul of to show him that the Gospel was only for the children of Israel, for the circumcised, not for the gentiles. But Paul did not fear conflicts with his brothers, he listened fully to the voice that spoke to him in his soul, he believed more in the present than in the past, and so he "saved" that first community, helping it to rise again, using his "charisma" to add new narrative capital to the first immense story, making it even more immense. Paul's stories and tales are not only, and not above all, the stories and tales of Christ's historical life: *They are the stories and words of Paul*, which have also served the stories of Christ's life that came after him, and which perhaps would not have reached us, or would not have had the infinite strength that they had and still have without Paul's tenacious fidelity to his own different narrative capital. If communities only had the "Peters", they would not save themselves from the obsolescence of their own narrative capital. The arrival of new "Pauls" is perhaps the only true salvation for the VBOs. But when we are in labour, we cannot know it, we can only hope and pray for it, and we can stay with the "lamps lit" to try to recognize when and if it arrives. And even if it does not arrive, we can live well and for a long time even if we wait for a true hope, renouncing to console ourselves with false hopes.

Real expectations are a precious nourishment of real life. There are VBOs that end their race because they do not let Paul arrive. Others cannot recognize it because they have turned off their lamps. Others because give the name of Paul to the first false prophet passing by, a seller of cheap and easy salvations. Resurrections are not contracts. Nobody can assure us that they will come. On the contrary, what makes the miracle of their arrival is precisely the very real possibility that it will never happen. Non-false resurrections are always a gift, and therefore unforeseen. Only then do they surprise us and leave us breathless when they happen. When we recognize that wonderful voice in the person we thought was just a gardener.

The road to Damascus is normal

Narrative capitals are pluralistic. Not all the stories they are composed of have the same value. Only a few are able to carry the weight of the new construction. "Wheat" and "weeds" are found in all fields of the earth, including those special fields where our ideals grow. At the beginning, we must grow all the plants in the field, because – as the great evangelical metaphor says – if the peasants intervened to eradicate the weeds, they would also tear away the good and precious ears of wheat.

Preserving all the ears of good wheat is a vital duty and a moral imperative of the founders and the first generation of a community and a VBO, and this rightful concern to preserve the entirety of the experience and its narrative capital means that when the foundation phase ends, the harvest includes good wheat mixed with the weeds. So the heritage that the founders leave us is always a legacy of wheat *and* couch grass.

Some organizations become extinct because, already in the original phase, they do not know how to live with the presence of weeds and the inevitable impurity of incarnations. So they try to immediately separate the bad grasses from the good ones and do not allow all the seeds to reach ripeness. Also because, unlike the real seeds and fields, the genuine components of our ideals can be distinguished from the bad ones only with the passing of time, and often what seemed to be discordant at the beginning, later flourished in wheat, and vice versa. Ideals grow well only by getting contaminated by all the nearby vegetation. They nourish off the same substances, live in osmosis with very different trees and, sometimes, also with poisonous fungi (that are only poisonous for those who eat them, but not for the other plants). Sometimes these flowers and plants are so delicate that they can grow only because they are protected by the shadow of less noble trees that, however, are more resistant to scorching heat. Only bonsai trees can live in the sterile places of our living rooms. They do not bear fruit, they have no roots and they do not grow. Real stories are written with entire chapters of novels written by others and with passages of myths of surrounding "pagan cults". No narrative capital is entirely new. Most of its ideas and stories are *inheritance*, even when the writer of a new story is not fully aware of them (because he or she fears that recognizing the gift of the past reduces novelty). Whoever begins to live and tell a community, corporate or political, a story *inherits* and *generates* wheat and weed.

But – and this is the most delicate and crucial process – those who come after the foundation phase tend almost inevitably to identify weeds *only in the first inheritance*, i.e. in the ideas and stories that the founders found as materials that existed prior to their new house, and to consider all good wheat that was produced by the founder. They thus attempt a first separation by looking for weeds only "outside" and "earlier", not "inside" and "during" the original words of the founder. In some cases, we end up writing a new narrative capital by completely eliminating the old "contaminated" stories inherited from the past and the environment, composing new stories using only what we think is new and original of the available materials. And so the weeds also present within the new ideas and stories of foundation grow undisturbed because *they are confused with wheat*. Until one day the good fruits (new members and vocations) are finished, suffocated by weeds disguised as wheat.

Sometimes, at this stage of narrative famine, the post-foundation community has the gift and strength to realize that if it nurtures the hope of saving itself, it must courageously begin the separation of wheat/weeds, even inside the original narrative capital of the founder. Usually, it is not without internal resistance that they begin to have a more mature and "distant" look at the ideas, writings and stories of the foundation in search of really good wheat.

But even in these necessary steps it is very easy to find ourselves having exchanged the weeds with wheat. This is due to a very common mistake. It is thought that the true and good part of the narrative capital lies in its most *spectacular and sensational* elements, and so the more sober, simpler, poorer and more ordinary components are torn away. It is a serious and widespread error, especially in the experiences born of spiritual and religious charismas. In these founding stories there are events, key episodes and narrations that were most impressive for the imagination of the founders themselves and later for the feelings of their first followers. They are often linked to facts that lie at the boundary between the natural and the supernatural, between the ordinary and the miraculous. In some cases, they take the form of stories of visions or special revelations and, in general, they seem to be secret, often Gnostic and mysterious.

Each foundation, especially if it originates from a rich and deep charisma, is surrounded by this narrative component. Even the Church of the early days, for example, abounded in such stories, of which it also nourished and enriched itself. The time came, however, when the first Christians had to govern the proliferation of this spectacular and miraculous narrative component. Thus, among the many stories that circulated in those second and third phases, only four Gospels and few other texts were chosen. Today we know that some (perhaps many) episodes and words contained in the apocryphal and Gnostic Gospels were no less "true" than the facts and words preserved in canonical texts. Many tales bloomed in a period farther from the first historical events, when some began to think that the first sober and essential *kerygma* was not spectacular and secret enough to convert and conquer. But without that effort of separation and discernment, the primitive Church would have been devoured by its own stories. The most sensational part that circulated about the life of Jesus and the apostles would have eaten up the overly sober stories of a young woman from Nazareth, the beatitudes for the poor and the afflicted, the story of the passion and therefore of the resurrection, which would have been equated to the many miracles of Jesus, to the ones that were similar to the deeds of the false prophets and magicians, or to the "resurrection" of Lazarus. In the abundance of extraordinary stories, those first communities had to "sacrifice" some real or probable facts, in order to save the novelty of their own story capable of generating present and future. It is surely no coincidence that the resurrection of Jesus was accompanied by very few descriptions. The scene includes a few frightened women, a young man wearing white clothes, a gardener – incredulous people. The oldest manuscripts of the oldest Gospel ended with these beautiful words, commenting on the empty tomb seen by the women: "and they said nothing to anyone" (Mark, 16:8). In Paul's letters, there are no stories of the miracles of Jesus, only that of a "miracle" of a crucified-and-risen person who is alive and is met by others along the way.

In moments of crisis of stories to tell, it is too easy to think that today's new stories will have to start from the most striking stories of yesterday. We deceive ourselves if we believe that talking about past miracles is enough to generate new "miracles" that would be needed today to continue the journey, and are missing. As if to revive the original reality it was enough to simply *remember* the special deeds of yesterday, and not relive them. We fall into a *consumerist syndrome*, which is as likely and tempting and as rich of special events that the foundation was, and we run the risk of blocking the next generation in the *gluttonous* consumption of sterile memories. Another *resource curse*: The more colourful the past is, the more faded the present risks of becoming since the present is then lived by *consuming the past*, forgetting the future. Here the fatal error lies in the lack of understanding that the special gifts received in the founding phase were only "the wedding gift" from which a beautiful (because ordinary and possible for all) new life was born. They are unique and unrepeatable experiences because they are linked to the revelation of the "prophetic" vocation of the founders. The fruitful inheritance that the founders leave us is not only dowry received as a gift, but the life born of those weddings. It is a living child, not a shimmering, sterile diamond.

When this error occurs, the extraordinary part of the narrative capital, which is also part of the inheritance, becomes "bad money", not because it is bad or false in itself, but because, in a new version of the old *Gresham's Law*, it "drives out" the "good money" of the hard work of those who are seriously and humbly trying to write a new beautiful normality in life after the crisis of the first stories. This work of writing generative narrative capital is thwarted by the sellers of the *memories*, special effects and fireworks of the early days that are no longer there. It was not the big grey dog appearing to Don Bosco that generated the great Salesian educational movement; it was born above all from the very average "whistle" that the young John Bosco provoked from the youngster named Bartolomeo. It was not the events recorded in "Fioretti" or the stigmata of Saint Francis that generated and regenerated the Franciscan movement, but the radical and tenacious fidelity of Francis to the "Madonna of Poverty" of the Gospel. Isaiah did not save and nourish his people with the story of the vision of seraphim in the Temple on the day of his vocation, but with the humble prophecy of a child and a small faithful remnant, which fuelled non-vain hope during the exile, and which today continues to nourish our love-filled waiting that never ends.

The sensational and extraordinary experiences of the foundation are *beautiful seeds, but they don't reproduce*, and they only tend to throw the VBO back into the past, to make it addicted to narcotic substances. The new good narrative capital is not that of the memories of the miracles of yesterday, but the one generated by the new tales of today's real and simple life.

In narrative capital crises there are always very few remaining resources. A VBO saves itself if it does not invest these in the consumption of its own extraordinary stories of the past, because it understands that the good wheat was to be found in the normal life of the first phase, in those facts that can still sprout many others *because they are so extraordinary as to be ordinary, so finite to be really infinite* – the story of a crucified man, a friend of sinners, fishermen, of those who forgive, of those who are forgiven, of communities that simply live in mutual love. It is still possible to fall off the horse, only on these normal and dusty roads of Damascus.

The naked freedom of the eyes

Ideology is a very common and serious illness in VBOs, and it develops especially during the crisis of narrative capital, when amidst the shortage of true stories to tell the offer of new artificial stories that seem to respond to the hunger for sense and future hitting the community becomes very seductive. Ideology is the *neurosis of the ideal* – just as idolatry is the neurosis of faith. Among the many forms that ideologies take, a particularly frequent and dangerous form is the one suggested by Spanish writer Don Juan Manuel's novel entitled *El Conde Lucanor* (*Tales of Count Lucanor*), which is the medieval source of the fairy tale *The Emperor's New Clothes*. But, unlike its various modern rewritings, in the original novel we find precious elements to add new words to our discourse on movements and communities that originate from ideals, charismas and motivations, which are different and larger than the economic ones.

The story begins with a bizarre deception suffered by a king. Three rogues come to court and promise him special clothes, which can only be seen by legitimate children, while remaining invisible to those who are illegitimate. The king takes the bait, since he believes he has found a good mechanism to prevent the inheritance of someone who would prove to be a non-natural son. So the three cheater tailors get to work. The king, still doubtful, sends two servants to see the first new clothes, without revealing anything about their supposed magical properties to them. The servants see nothing in the spinning mills, but they don't have the courage to contradict the tailors, and they tell the king that they saw wonderful fabrics. Finally, when the king also goes to the tailors to see their work and cannot see anything, at first, he is upset but then he thinks, "If I say I can't see the clothes, everyone will know that I'm not the king's son, and I will lose my kingdom". So he believes the trick and he too begins to weave his praises of the new garments. Then he sends his governor, who, having heard about the features of those clothes from the king, even though he cannot see anything praises them with even more enthusiastic words, in order not to lose his position. After the governor, the other court officials also do the same. And when the feast day finally arrives and the king, completely naked, rides through the streets of the city on horseback, all the people praise the king's beautiful clothes. The spell is broken by a stableman of the king who says, "My Lord, for me it is the same thing to be the son of my father or another, and for this reason I say to you: either I am blind or you are naked".

In this type of ideological production, first there are cheating *false prophets* that seduce the boss – the founder(s) or leader(s) of a community. It is not him calling them, but he receives them, and in doing so he commits the first and decisive mistake. From the cheater false prophets, we should defend ourselves first of all by not receiving them at home and by making sure that they do not pass the controls that we normally do before receiving guests. During the storytelling crises, when numerous storytellers are asking to be received, it is essential to choose the "doorkeepers" carefully, that is to say those who welcome visitors, the staff of the executive or bureau secretariat. They play a very important role, because they must have the rare ability to spot false prophets immediately and block them. Because, in crises affecting the deep meaning of the community, those responsible are particularly manipulable by storyteller false prophets, by ideological snake charmers. Many crises are not overcome insofar as the secretariat allows the wrong storytellers to pass through or because it blocks the good ones – or it does both.

It was not by chance that at the head of the guest quarters of the abbeys and monasteries there were very wise and expert monks and friars: "Moreover, let also a God-fearing brother have assigned to him the apartment of the guests" (*Holy Rule of Saint Benedict*, chapter LIII). In delicate moments of transition, wise communities must understand which the offices and functions are decisive. These almost never follow the formal order of the organization chart. In a good organization, the morphology of power does not coincide with the morphology of wisdom; and if wiser people are all placed in the senior positions, the others find themselves in the suburbs, which are the places of "weak powers" where the most serious diseases penetrate. Peripheral wisdom is always decisive, but especially when you are surrounded by false storytellers in search of "kings" to enchant. Also because the leaders of spiritual and religious VBOs who are faced with very delicate crises of stories to tell, essential in order to be able to enchant the present and future members once again, are particularly exposed to the narrative manipulation of false prophets. And the more serious, widespread and profound narrative crisis that one goes through, the easier it is for founders and decision-makers to believe in the fantastic promises of the deceitful storytellers. "Kings" are always very sensitive to the inheritance of their kingdom. They have a vital need to understand who the legitimate children of their "charisma" are. And when, in times of crisis, they can no longer simply recognize them with their gaze, they are extremely vulnerable to those who promise them techniques that replace their eyes – communities are lost when false prophets prevent their founders/leaders from understanding who the authentic followers of their real history are.

Furthermore, it is important to note that in the story the deception could have been discovered immediately if one of the servants whom the (still doubtful) king sent for a first verification of the clothes had the freedom and courage to simply say what he saw, without fearing the costs and punishment for the freedom of his eyes. But it is precisely this kind of brave and free members who are scarce in the "secretariats" and around the founders and leaders. Almost always, thus, they end up surrounded by "servants", who are very faithful but without the freedom and courage to simply say the things they see. They are even good persons, but they are moved and manipulated by their fear, even when it is disguised as respect or even veneration for their leaders. It is precisely in the first relationship between the servants sent out and the king where ideology is formed and begins to work. It is not enough to deceive the head. Ideology is a relationship; it is a "relational evil" that requires two or more people who begin to believe *together in the same illusion and say that they believe in it*. Ideology is a false individual belief that succeeds in becoming a collective belief, said loudly and in public – it is not enough to believe in ideologies, in order for them to get established they must also be proclaimed and repeated publicly and reciprocally.

Another decisive role is played by governors and ministers. These are initially not so much driven by fear (perhaps partly), but by interests. They, too, do not tell the truth, *although they know that they are telling a lie* – however, quite simply, they *have the incentive to lie*. At this point the ideological apparatus is already working, and it spreads in the population simply by replicating the same fear and the same interests. In true stories, however, there is a fundamental difference when comparing to the story narrated by the fairy tale. In real community affairs there are many people who are *able to really see the clothes that do not exist*. Ideology can become so powerful that we see a naked king as if he were dressed. And when the proportion of blind people in good faith exceeds that of those who lie (out of fear and interest), the ideological trap becomes (almost) perfect. We lose contact with reality because we can no longer distinguish what we really see from what we see thanks to the ideology. We live, even for a long time, in a false reality that some people – naively and sincerely – can really see and that others – out of interest – *say they see* knowing that they do not see it. The perfect producer-consumers of ideology are those who believe that the artificial world they see is really the true one – like *The Truman Show*, it is the perfect reality show that every TV would like, where the protagonist lives his or her false life convinced that it is his or her real life.

In Juan Manuel's story, there is a servant to break the spell who, says the fairy tale, "had nothing to lose". Having nothing to lose, and perhaps inspired by a little bit of goodwill for the deceived king, that stableman found himself in the conditions of freedom to be able to simply tell the truth. In the fairy tale the king "cursed that servant" who revealed the truth, but the other fellow citizens of the kingdom, one after the other, came out of the spell and deception, triggered an opposite chain reaction, and the swindlers fled, betaking themselves to their heels. But why, unlike in fairy tales, does human history show us very few cases of ideal-driven communities that manage to get out of the ideological spell? Those who really saw wonderful clothes thanks to their ideology-influenced eyes do not want to go back to a reality which is true but much less colourful than what they "saw" for a long time and to which they were addicted – as a matter of fact, ideology is a form of doping which guarantees exceptional performance and removes the incentive to return to the fatigue and sweat of practice in the uphill roads and of uncertain results. Furthermore, over the years, many of those who initially saw the invisible because of interest have gradually transformed themselves into honest seers, and the share of people who see non-existing things in good faith can become an almost totality. Finally, the very few who have remained conscious of the ideological bluff are also those who are earning most from that collective comedy. Ideology is also very dangerous because once activated it feeds on itself, in different but convergent ways.

However, the happy ending of the fairy tale contains a message of non-vain hope. It is not impossible that – even outside the world of fairy tales – a single person saves everyone. One of the "remnant", a person who saved the freedom of their heart and eyes during the time of illusions. Like Noah. There are certain crucial moments when the "critical mass" is "1". A single person who "has nothing to lose", because, perhaps, they have already given everything, or because they have managed to shield their poverty. The many forms of poverty usually reduce our freedom, but sometimes poverty alone can generate a different freedom that is capable of liberating others. And if we then realize that in our desolate land of these poor people there is not even one left, we can always hope to become that one ourselves.

The wings of life

Life, in its fullness, has the power to satisfy and satiate in itself. The moon, the dawn, the sunset, pain, love, a gaze, a child, are more concrete and true *incarnate words* than the words we use to describe them. If it were not so, we would not understand why most people, yesterday and today, do not know how to compose poems or theological essays, yet they can touch life at the same depth as a poet or a philosopher. It is this direct access to the mystery of existence that really makes us all equal under the sun, before the many differences and inequalities, whether they are good or bad. And this, perhaps, makes us able to feel, occasionally, a true universal fraternity with animals, plants and the earth, that we feel alive, just like ourselves. But, as it often happens, this infinite richness can also be transformed into a form of poverty, in some cases.

The primacy of life assumes a special force and scope in collective organizations generated by ideals and/or charismas. Life always comes first, but when that life fills itself with spirit and gives rise to a community of meaning, this experience can become so fulfilling that we believe that there is no need for more than the life we are already living.

When later life continues and communities grow thanks to that first beauty, there comes a time when we should start *thinking* about the beautiful things we are doing, and to do them well we need "beautiful" cultural categories like the life we are living. But often, dazed by the fullness of present life, one easily passes from the right and natural primacy of life to the absolutization of its experiential dimension and ends up preventing that same life from being expressed in all its beauty, strength and duration. The fullness of the present empties the future.

And it is precisely in this dynamic between 'only life' and life when often VBOs meet decisive challenges and pitfalls. Life suffices, it is true, but in collective ideal experiences life really suffices only if that *life becomes also culture*. History tells us that in order for a collective novelty to continue beyond the season of its foundation, it is not enough to continue living the novelty. It is also necessary to know how to think about it to be able to tell it with the right categories and words, which should contain the same degree of novelty as the actual experiences.

In the early days, the personality of the founders, the almost infinite vital energy and the blinding light of novelty manage to cover the need for suitable categories and language; for a long time, we live and grow convinced that there is no need for any cultural or theoretical work. But in reality, and from the outset, communities have to use categories and languages to live and speak. And so either they decide to try to "manufacture" the instruments they do not yet have, or they simply buy or borrow them. But the more original an experience is, the less good instruments already existing on the market will be found. Also because when a community novelty is born, that novelty is also a *novelty of life and culture*. But unlike 'only life', cultural novelties do not thrive spontaneously: there is a need for intentional and specific work to bring them to existence – and that rarely happens.

It should not be surprising then that the re-absorption of innovations generated by communities and ideal-driven movements in tradition is the most common outcome that historical evidence shows us, because the use of wrong and/or old categories found on the market simply results in the *downsizing* of the novelty experienced and lived. Bad culture chases good life away.

Today many spiritual communities (but also some beautiful civil enterprises and cooperatives) risk extinguishing themselves because they have not done a specific cultural work on their identity in the appropriate time, and, as they keep talking about their newness in a culturally bad way they are gradually losing strength on the level of life. The wrong cultural categories are transformed into a bed of Procrustes (a rogue smith from ancient Greek mythology who forced people to fit the size of an iron bed by stretching or cutting off their feet) where those novelties that do not fall within the overly narrow measures are amputated. And what's left out is necessarily the surplus between the old and the new, i.e. the greatest and most original innovations of which they were the bearers. For these (and other) reasons in ideal community experiences, the new wine of life ends up in old narrative wineskins and disperses. They are beautiful experiences – told with inappropriate languages.

Furthermore, there are some typical errors committed by those VBOs that have understood the importance of building new cultural categories. The first consists in confusing *cultural* categories and language with *spiritual* categories and language. A first work is started, but it stops too soon at the language and spiritual or religious principles, which are generally the first languages that are born together with the experience. However, cultural work would require transforming and universalizing both the experience and *its spiritual/religious language*, which in these cases does not occur because the input is confused with the output of the process. And so the novelty does not grow, as it is confined in places and languages that are too narrow for it.

Culture needs *spirit* and *flesh, the wholeness of life*, if that life is to grow and bear fruit. In this type of work, envisaging the appropriate time is crucial, because it is much more difficult to correct fake cultural categories than to start from scratch. And if a lot of time goes by, the borrowed categories are introduced into the flesh of the "charisma", and everything becomes too difficult.

A second mistake is to think that this cultural work should be entrusted to an elite of intellectuals or professors. This way one forgets that culture is much more than intellectual work because it needs the life and thought of every member of a community, including the life and thought of people, work or the poor. Categories and language that do not serve life are elaborated, and they end up only removing and discarding intellectually less well-equipped people and encouraging the creation of new castes.

Finally, there are communities that begin their work by defining a priori what the experts will have to study, in order to confirm and strengthen them culturally, but without calling it all into question. This work, therefore, is not done with the freedom of spirit that any true cultural work would require, and we end up reiterating only the pre-cultural beliefs that were already known, convinced that we have carried out a cultural work – that has never actually begun. In the history of Christianity, truths and dogmas have emerged at the end of a free and non-dogmatic cultural workplace that has lasted for centuries, from dialogue and harsh confrontation with heretics and schismatics, to the crucible of dialectics between very different visions. The accounts of the truths of the Christian faith have been many and varied since the beginning: four Gospels, Paul's letters together with those of James and Peter, in continuity with a Jewish Bible where Job and the Song of Songs, Daniel and Qoheleth coexisted. The Old and New Testament have not become a sterile ideology as they were multifold and pluralistic, because, using different voices and the tension among themselves; they have said truths that are greater and more complex than those possible for a single story. Without conflicts between Paul and Peter, which took place before the composition of the Gospels, those Gospels would have been much poorer and perhaps lost among the many ideological, apocalyptic and Gnostic texts of Palestine and Syria.

In many VBOs, on the other hand, we work on the cultural mediation of the ideal message with a *mandate of orthodoxy* for non-negotiable truths, and so the essential elaboration of language and categories ends up becoming a poor exercise, since it is homophonic, producing a shrinking of life instead of representing its universalization and blossoming. It becomes a leash that prevents the free flight of the charisma or confines it within the perimeter of its cage. One Gospel alone is not enough for a VBO to tell its miracle.

Good cultural work is never a mere translation of an already existing reality into an essentially identical reality, told in another language. This is typical of ideological operations and their "organic intellectuals". Cultural work is not a technique, but it is the *unveiling* of novelties that were not seen before and that would not be seen in its absence, it is *discovering* that the organizations that seem brand new were already present in tradition, it is the unmasking of the highly abundant ideological infiltrations in VBOs and that ideals and life end up suffocating without a systematic and free cultural exercise. Paul not only translated the first Christian proclamation, and similarly, Bonaventure and Thomas Aquinas did not simply translate the charismas of Saint Francis and Saint Dominic: They innovated and created realities that we would not have without their "charismas". They allowed the ideals of their founders to have larger wings so that they could fly higher upwards and reach to us. In every real cultural operation, there always hides the risk of heresy and betrayal, a risk that often stops the real and necessary cultural work from being born.

In order to try to explain the infinite novelty of the first Christmas night, it was not enough to tell the stories of the shepherds or those of Mary and the first disciples. Without new charismas, without time and much work, no one could have written that "the Word became flesh and dwelt among us". The gospel has been able to enchant and change the world because it is a *wonderful story*. The first *new* wineskin in the gospel is the gospel itself.

The desire for Christmas has never disappeared on Earth. It is we who have stopped telling its story for some time now, with the beauty necessary to enchant our colleagues, friends and children today. All they are waiting for is to be told, with new words, that God became a baby in a woman, that he was born poor in a cave, and was reborn from his tomb.

Fraternity has hands and feet

At the origins of many communities and movements, there is an experience of intense and deep closeness, among all of the members and – in the first place – with the founders. It is an extended kind of intimacy that exalts and develops the intimacy of each person. This particular "relational good" attracts, fills and fascinates no less than the ideal message received and announced. The contact of hearts and bodies, the sharing of the same table where meals prepared together are eaten, the real hugs to the "lepers" that immediately become true and different hugs exchanged with each other upon returning home. These are radically *anti-immunitarian* experiences, precisely because the many forms of mediation that we have invented in order not to touch the "wound of the other" are not there yet.

But this simple and universal proximity-fraternity is the first to be jeopardized when communities create a structure for themselves and become increasingly complex organizations. In this transformation of the nature of relationships, some of the most devious and bad viruses are nestled.

The evolution of *relationships with the founders* plays a key role. Soon after the first phase of fraternity and horizontality, an increasing *distance is* created between the founders and other members, and the intimate proximity of the origin is progressively reduced. It becomes increasingly more difficult to see the founders simply in the midst of the community, to meet them in the street, to share ordinary life with them. And so, paradoxically, it is precisely the founders who are the first to emerge from the reciprocity-fraternity that is sincerely believed and proclaimed. Their different and unique role, which everyone recognizes, generates an invisible but very real and ever more impenetrable curtain around them, which produces a real and actual *isolation*, which grows together and thanks to admiration, sincere love and the exaltation of their person.

And many ideal communities are *intentionally* transformed into immunitarian organizations, given that with distance the experience of *corporeality*, contact, full human encounter and *intimacy* in relationships also disappears. We can speak and announce fraternity and equality, but if we do not embrace, quarrel and forgive each other mixing the flow of our tears, we are in the *ideology* of fraternity without entering into the *experience* of fraternity. The body, as biblical humanism tells us, expresses concreteness, fragility, the entirety of life, it allows us to know the mystery of the person I am facing here and now. If I do not meet the other in their body, I see only an indistinct crowd, categories and classes of people, without being able to "see" Giovanna, Ivan, Luca. I "meet" but a ghost, even when it is a beautiful ghost. To *recognize* him or her, I must be able to touch his or her wounds with my hands. Here lies the immense meaning of a word that becomes flesh.

This is why a first sign that a fraternal community is turning into an immune organization is the decrease in the exposure of those responsible for it to the wounds (and blessings) of the simple fraternity of all.

This is how one affirms, day after day, one of the oldest and most universal taboos: "You cannot touch the king", a taboo that comes from a powerful desire for the forbidden thing. The taboo is affirmed together with the growing of the distance from the founder, it is all the more difficult to "touch him". The growth of the myth is proportional to the decrease in encounters, hugs and kisses given to the lepers throughout the community – which, in rare cases of pathology, can also be accompanied by the *abuse* of bodies, a sick expression of the actual eclipse of the real body. The real antidote to this taboo would therefore be to maintain the intimacy and ordinary closeness between the founders and the whole community. But this is precisely the most difficult thing to avoid, because myths are nourished precisely by their being far from reality – an encounter and a look at the leader is as valuable as distant and unattainable he is (we also see this in the case of the "myths" of cinema and music).

These growing processes of isolation and untouchability have some *inevitable* and also some *avoidable* components, but the management of their avoidable part is decisive, also because some avoidable dimensions are interpreted as unavoidable. Among these, thinking that the distance and loss of intimacy with the founders depends on the quantitative growth of the community, without realizing that the first ones to become distant are those closest to the founder, because the "distance" is above all sacred and symbolic, not geographical. The "neighbour" is not the "next-door neighbour" – as the good Samaritan taught us.

The inevitable part is a consequence of the success of communities. An awareness of the uniqueness and value of the founder's person pushes members to do everything possible to protect them so as to save them from being "consumed" by the people around them. Furthermore, growth and development necessarily produce some form of structures and hierarchy, which by their nature and function combine poorly with what is needed for fraternity. This inevitably implies the emergence of a culture of distance that becomes immunity. This is a paradox as well known as it is neglected by the founders of charismatic communities and movements, who generally make great haste to start the phase of institutionalizing their groups (and even when they are abstractly aware of it, they believe, deceiving themselves, that their story will be special and different and *therefore* will not run into the problems of others). A good warning to community founders could then be summed up as follows: Instead of *accelerating it*, as you spontaneously do, try to do everything you can to slow down the process of transforming your community into an organization. Move yourself like the equilibrist (tightrope walker) without haste. Do not get caught up by the call of the other end of the rope.

The avoidable factors concern the founder directly. First of all, it should resist with all its virtues the tenacious temptation of isolation, especially when it is about to start and is more easily visible. It should not stop being present by the tables where all people eat, in the masses, continuing to embrace and kiss the real poor, not only those of the stories. It should not fall into the invisible trap of (always less and small) privileges, *exemptions* from the work and duties of everyone – like washing dishes, shopping, ironing shirts. Fraternity begins to become an ideology when it loses contact with chopping the onions and cleaning the toilets; when the desire to "give life" to the brothers does not become "swiping the floor" with a cloth.

It is very difficult for the founders not to fall into these forms of exemptions, which are the result of very good intentions, a great deal of love and an ignorance that is not guilty of the consequences. It is, in fact, the community that, in good faith, does everything to isolate its leader. *It is Peter who does not want Jesus to wash his feet.* But when another Peter succeeds in convincing his master and thus impedes the fraternity of hands and feet, the great and ancient taboo of the king's untouchability becomes, day after day, the real new tacit rule of the community. Few things isolate more from friends and companions than those that, instead of helping the founders/ leaders to remain *equal* to all, make them increasingly *different*. Those, however, who have received a charisma of founding a community would have a vital need of honest *friends* who like them so much as to treat them as equals, because they understand that the best way to help them play their different and special role is to keep them in ordinary and normal relationships, to contradict them, correct them, not to say "yes" to them at all times, not to rob them of the proximity of fraternity.

Unlike all empires and today's capitalist enterprises (where the untouchability of leaders is a common rule, and where one arrives at self-destruction because of the excess of immunity), communities and ideal movements cannot afford this taboo, because an "untouchable king" inevitably produces crisis and, if untreated, the death of the organization-community.

Because though at first this immunity-related disease acts on the relationship between members and their "head", it soon becomes the paradigm of every relationship. That partial and distant relationality, without intimacy and emotions, extends and reproduces itself on all hierarchical levels, and infects all private relationships. And so the exemptions and privileges extend to all the various "leaders", and the apathetic and bodiless relationality takes root throughout the community and becomes a general and widespread culture. One begins not by "touching" the founder, but by not touching any leaders, and ends up not touching anybody – not even one's own interiority, which becomes increasingly distant and poor. Because when you lose contact with the other's body – since all distances increase – you become less and less able to feel life, to take your own and others' limits, or the imperfections and sins of history seriously, to cultivate emotions and desires, to develop that human *pietas* that can only grow in the impurity of concrete life. And you find yourself in an atrophy of real human emotions and feelings, replaced by artificial emotions and feelings because they are all "bodiless". It is not at all rare to meet communities, especially in the generations after their foundation, which speak of an abstract solidarity and reciprocity, because the real ones have been "devoured" over time by the sacred culture of immunity and non-contact. The "heart of flesh" needs bodies that grow in the only good life possible: That of all women and men "under the sun". I have been to funerals where the priests and nuns who were relatives of the deceased, were the least able to cry and feel a sincere *pieta*.

It is very difficult to defeat this community illness, not least because it is often mistaken for health. But it is not impossible. Sometimes, you can find a way out of the myth and realize that you are ill. However, the cure is far from easy. We would need the courage to identify the disease of *immunitas* in the original nucleus of the first narrative capital, because the virus begins to work in the lives of the founders very soon, and therefore it is also found in the stories that constitute the first inheritance. But the "untouchability of the king" over time has become a tacit norm so deeply rooted that it also impedes the *touchability of his narrative capital*. And so we work on the peripheral aspects of "charisma" and tradition, without touching their heart; and the virus continues to act and to reproduce.

The cure would consist in the ability to re-found a new capital by drawing on the pre-immune phase of the experience, when everyone was still free and simple. And from there, to re-read all the other stories, which should not be discarded but only understood and loved in their embodied corporeality (taking the body seriously means understanding and loving the illnesses of our history, as well). And so the true miracle of reciprocity in time and between generations would be fulfilled: To restore to our founders the fraternity that we stole from them yesterday.

Authenticity cannot be simulated

Every organization and every community would like to have members who authentically identify with their institutional mission, genuinely love its narratives and truly believe in what they say and do. This difficult operation of sincere individual identification with the institutional mission succeeds very well in the context of VBOs, especially when ideals are so high that they puncture the sky and let us glimpse paradise. This creates a perfect synergy between the individual and the community. Everyone believes, hopes, loves and desires the things of all others, without this "socialization of the heart" being experienced as the alienation and expropriation of the hearts of individuals.

As a matter of fact, when visiting such communities, one is struck by this dilated inner life that can be breathed and touched. What we see is a human group, but the impression we have is a sense of meeting one person who *subsists* in the many people. An unmistakable community style is created, a collective personality that communicates itself in language, interior design, collective rituals, artistic expressions and even somatic traits. Everyone tells the same story, honestly.

There is a phase of life, usually the first and second youth, when the individual person experiences the same *me/us* (i.e. the unity of the personal/collective levels) with immense enthusiasm and a feeling of great fullness, without any problematic notes. They do not notice anything non-authentic in feeling, thinking and speaking with the thoughts and words of the community, because they sincerely feel all of it their own and live them as a very intimate experience. No ideal path would begin without this kind of spiritual and anthropological *transubstantiation*, a form of "mystical union" between the individual and the collective soul. The *ideal us* naturally and joyfully becomes the *ideal me*. You feel at home only when you align your feelings with those of everyone, when the mutual inhabitation of emotions touches perfection. One suffers and rejoices for the same things and in the same way, everyone prays with the same words, reads (almost) the same words of the Bible, the same words as the founders. It is the presence of this phase of a totally free, intimate, sincere and very generous adherence of the soul to its own community that tells the essence of that mysterious reality that we call "vocation".

When a community or organization is born, its greatest heritage is precisely the existence of many people who, sincerely and authentically, live this coincidence between *me* and *us*. They are convincing and win many others because they truly and totally believe in the message they announce. The exponential growth that many ideal communities experience in the early days depends very much on the perfect identification of the *me* of individuals with the communitarian us – one of the most exciting experiences of the human repertoire.

This stage is never short; it can last many years. *However, it must not last forever.* Because if at some point it does not end, it turns from being a "blessing" into a "curse". The splendid youth of vocations gives the gift of its pearl only if it is able to die. However, many, too many times, the experience of youth does not end; it lasts for life and generates one of the most serious and frequent collective diseases.

Becoming an adult is difficult for everyone, but it is really difficult (and wonderful) when we spend a wonderful vocational youth with our *me* truly becoming *us*. Many times, in fact, we get crushed by the enormous richness of the first beautiful phase of the new life – another expression of the now known "curse of abundance". Those who manage the communities fall in love and then become too accustomed to the infinite availability of the moral energy of youth, and, more or less unconsciously, do everything so that it lasts as long as possible. Furthermore, individuals do not have "incentives" to get out of this form of childhood, where they feel just fine. The balance is therefore perfect and stable. And so too many people remain adolescents throughout their lives, believing, perhaps, that they have reached the peaks of spiritual life, because they are confused by the plastic toy peaks. Childlike spirit is not anthropological and psychological childhood, but the summit of an adult life that returns to being a child in a different way, not on purpose. The main problem of many communities is that they have too many quiet people who can't even reach the anthropological stage of the conflict between the *me* and the *us* (not to mention overcoming it). The first indicator of the maturity and freedom of an ideal-driven community and of the quality of its people is the presence of people in crisis for this same reason, struggling for a new kind of maturity. Again, the seriousness of the disease lies in confusing health with illness.

Sometimes, it happens that some people manage to reach the phase of crisis, and the *me-us* (individual-collective) harmony begins to waver. These people have preserved some living desire, they have been able to cultivate readings that are different from those of everyone, they have not lost contact with the real wounds of the real poor, they have not broken up with yesterday's friends, they have continued to pray with the old prayers of their grandmothers and not only with the new and special ones. These people can receive the great blessing of being able to become adults.

But, even in these happy cases, the management of these blessing-crises is rarely good. The highest obstacles are found inside the person, who when perceiving the first cracks of the inviolable block of the first intimacy and identity, denies and rejects them. People do not want to see this because, paradoxically, instead of interpreting these divergent symptoms as the beginning of a new authenticity, they experience them as non-authenticity and non-truth. It frightens them very much, and they halt. Moreover, in addition to the subjective feeling of *inauthenticity* and betrayal that holds the person back, there is the other, very high obstacle represented by those responsible who, in good faith, often recommend the return to the previous phase of harmony and peace. They fail to recognize the blessing in the first symptoms of this type of crisis, and they fight them.

The vast majority of possible crises abort before they are born; they are rejected and declined as temptation or betrayal – an infinite and immeasurable waste of human values, oceans of pain.

Also because – and here is a decisive point – from the day after the arrival of the first cracks, returning to the first peaceful and sincere authenticity is impossible. The first crisis is a point of no return, one can, one must, go only ahead. Every return becomes, this time really, *inauthentic*. People are no longer able to laugh, rejoice or pray like they did in the early days. They are laughs and prayers similar to those of yesterday, but they are no longer the same. And so to try to bridge the gap between what you *really* hear and say and what you *almost really* hear and say, you start to simulate some of your emotions and feelings. The phase of false authenticity has begun.

Sometimes, the growing of this gap produces a new crisis, which generally ends like the first one, with a new reversal that is done in a less and less convinced and more and more sorrowful way. People who are really convinced of the *us* live together in the communities alongside those who are less and less convinced but behave *as if* they were really convinced. But when the share of the "as if" exceeds that of the really convinced, the decline is rapid, because the spiritual and moral energies of partial authenticity are much smaller, and their ability to attract new members is even less. Simulated authenticity does not last long, and it consumes people's soul, to the point of extinguishing them. Many people leave communities (even when they formally remain there) because they are exhausted by these simulation exercises. Because if the part of false authenticity does not evolve by elaborating a new synthesis of the first *us*, it ends up infecting the part of sincere faith in the original message that had remained, to the point of not believing in it anymore (many people deny ideals of their youth to which they have not given the possibility of thriving, and so they have become trivial). Many spiritual communities and VBOs do not reach a second generation after their foundation because, collectively, they cannot overcome this first infinite youth, and the *us* of childhood – the genuine and the simulated version of it – devours the possible and beautiful us of adult life.

Some rare times, however, a second (or umpteenth) crisis manages to finally generate a new life, a new individual and collective spirit. And when it happens, the most beautiful years of life begin. If it is true that there are few things sadder than a beautiful youthful vocation that has withered being unable to mature, it is even truer that very few things are more beautiful than a person who has managed to generate a new *us* by bringing their *first me* and *first us* with them. But there would be a need for responsible leaders who have experienced this alchemy themselves and are therefore able to create the conditions for people to reach at least the phase of tension between *me* and *us*, that is to say, the phase of cracks in the wall. To help their people to get out of the safe land of the first collective authenticity, accepting and loving the inevitable and concrete risk that their exit will land them in distant places, that some of them will never return home. To understand that in order to have adult people, able to continue and enrich the collective history one day, they must put them in a position to make their *us* today die so that perhaps a new *us* may rise up tomorrow. To allow people to develop their talents, ambitions, desires, relationships and dreams that are different from those of everyone. To give them the chance to grow up differently, to imagine paths of *being adult* that are different from those imagined and dreamed of by young people and by everyone. The *us* of adult life are always plural and diverse, but no less real and faithful. However, in ideal communities the radical need to control the inner life of people out of (a more radical) fear of "losing" them once they become adults makes youth eternal and therefore degenerates it. And so they cannot even generate that "faithful remnant", the only ones capable of saving all the people tomorrow, who, in order to be generated, need freedom, open air and the biodiversity of fertile land – "whoever would save his life will lose it".

An entire community can be saved by *a single person* who has found a new adult authenticity. Someone who believed in a dream, found a wonderful child, felt "a great joy" – a new and different joy that they would never have known if they had stopped walking in pursuit of a star.

3   Surpluses and misalignments

The several colours of the swan

The "black swan" is that highly improbable event with very relevant effects whose arrival could be neither foreseen nor explained on the basis of the facts of the past. The expression comes from the discovery of black swans in Australia, which disproved the thesis that had been considered certain: "All swans are white". In fact, the black swan is the great enemy of companies and organizations, too, because of its potentially devastating effects.

But even if the more or less scientific debate that has developed in recent years highlights almost exclusively the destructive effects; in reality the totally unexpected and surprising events can also represent salvation for organizations and communities. The unexpected can be the greatest gift – we see it every day in our children. In fact, if we look deeply into the dynamics of actual organizations, whether economic or other, we realize that the real big enemy, the evil black swan is the invincible tendency to create rigid management routines built on the observation of the past, and therefore to prevent the understanding of the arrival of great novelties. By looking back, the management guiding today lets us "know" only what we have already known; theirs is a retroactive look that, as in the biblical story of Lot's wife (Genesis 19:26), transforms life into a dead statue of salt. Hence, the really serious danger for organizations does not lie in the existence of black swans but in their management, which is too often wrong.

The most common mistake comes from the fear of the arrival of the evil black swan that leads to hostility towards each swan with not-exactly white coloured feathers. Because of the terror of a black swan, everyone is left in the routine and monotony of a single-coloured world, and beauty and biodiversity are lost. It's an understandable choice, because if the unexpected event is one of the really bad ones, it can even lead to the *destruction* of the community by itself.

But it is precisely here that we enter the heart of one of the main paradoxes of communities (and people). The swan with different feathers that can be glimpsed on the horizon could be Satan or the Antichrist, but that strange colour could also be that of Isaiah, Francis and Clare, Teresa of Calcutta or Jesus of Nazareth. We can't know at first glance, nor at the second – often only at the end (that's where its tremendous and wonderful mystery lies). But if we block all the non-conforming colours in their auroral moment, perhaps we prevent the arrival of the devastating black swan (although we have no guarantee of success), but we certainly prevent the real and good news from coming, ripening and bringing their fruits and essential oils. One of the relational traps that make organizations much less creative, vital and innovative than they could be is in fact the more or less conscious struggle between the management and potential black swans. The former does everything to make the latter return to the routine logic – the sofas so commonly present in the halls of modern organizations are just like *beds of Procrustes*. Real innovation is linked to people who, to let them act to their full potential, cannot be managed with the typical managerial tools. Today we are finally realizing that vital organizations capable of generating real novelties *must renounce the same claim to govern and control their people*, because in truly decisive dynamics people are unmanageable, because if they were totally governed, they would lose the most innovative component of their creativity. The metaphor of the black swan is therefore a good rhetorical expedient to begin a discussion on the management of real *novelties* in organizations, people and governance rules.

What we have just pointed out becomes really decisive in the values-based organizations (VBOs). They are not *always* good and wonderful things, but they are *often* good and wonderful. In my homeland the *first* and often only capital consists in the people and their relational assets; all people, but especially those who act on the basis of intrinsic motivations; that is, those members, workers and managers who have not entered their respective organization primarily for economic and financial incentives, but because of an inner call, therefore by "vocation" (using this word, as always, in the most secular and broadest possible sense). VBOs continue after their foundation only if they are able to attract and retain a nucleus of people who know how to revive the first ideals. If, that is, they succeed in attracting, maintaining, cultivating and flourishing *at least one good black swan*, which will perhaps be able to revive the heritage passed down by the first generation.

And that's where the more important kind of reasoning begins.

In the meantime, there is a first fact: Many VBOs are born from black swan phenomena. The first one is the *founder him/herself*, because perhaps there is nothing more unpredictable and unexpected than the vast impact of the advent of a new charisma on Earth (including artistic charismas). Often the founder of a new community is a different swan that has flown away from an original community that, by mistake or by a new vocation, has become too confined a space for its higher and crazier flights.

During the foundation phase the innovative power of the founder is so extraordinary that it contaminates all the other members of the VBO, which gradually becomes a community of swans with the same plumage as the founder. The innovative dimension present in many members of the VBO is oriented towards the founder, and all their ideal energies and talents are used in a camouflaging way, to align themselves with the new "colour". This process works out very well, because the members of that community do not feel anything more intimate, sincere, true and proper than wanting to take on the features and tones of the founders.

That's how the founder's original diversity and their first *hetero-doxy* gradually generate a *new kind of orthodoxy*, and the founder's innovative colour gradually becomes the only colour for everyone. In the beginning, this operation of mimesis fully satisfies body and soul. But, without wanting or knowing it, this process ends up producing a static situation which is very similar, if not identical, to those realities that the founder and his followers wanted to change at the beginning. And so the heterodoxy generated by a black swan event that had criticized and forced the ancient dogma reproduces a new dogma during the life cycle of the founder that, like all dogmas, fights innovations. This dynamic, well known in the social and organizational sciences, is very often what marks the end of innovative and prophetic experiences, which exhaust their mission when they reach a situation similar to that from which they started.

In addition, VBOs attract many more potential black swans than other organizations, because ideal motivations, not to mention religious ones, select many excellent people in some dimensions. The VBOs have always been and continue to be populated by ethically and spiritually extraordinary people. For this reason a person who has received an authentic vocation (and every VBO, to be and to remain one, must host at least one) is *potentially a black swan*, because they are unique, unrepeatable and non-programmable. Neither they nor anyone else knows what they will become; nobody knows what impact their life will have on those of others: It is a message entrusted to a bottle and the sea that will be read only if and when someone picks it up (an argument that may well be valid for every person that comes into this world). Every vocation is a black swan event – unpredictable, unexpected and with great effects.

However, in the VBOs this is more radically present than elsewhere (the reasons for which will be analyzed in this series of articles); the management of radically innovative people is particularly difficult, painful and rarely crowned with success. A VBO knows or senses that in every different plumage the killer swan may be hiding, and this legitimate fear often devours the fulfilment of the promise, because the price of the hope of being able to generate a new authentic prophet is the possibility of generating ten false prophets. This radical fear can be overcome by giving the promise a much higher value than the fear of being killed by a particularly bad false prophet – an infinite value. So the hostility and resistance that every black swan process is met with in every organization are amplified and radicalized in the VBOs. The existence of a founding charisma/ideal naturally leads VBOs to be anchored in the past, to give more importance to the beginning than to the *eschaton*. This looking to the origin is part of the charismatic DNA of the VBOs, especially those of spiritual and religious nature. The eventual reformer could save them by moving the axis from the past to the future, but this is precisely what the charismatic communities and ideals most fear and fight against. We are inside a typical tragedy – but tragedies are also among the greatest creations of the human genius. Ordinary organizations, as they are often pragmatic and concrete, are more open to the new than VBOs. On the other hand, VBOs naturally develop powerful mechanisms to intercept and block the arrival of bad black swans. However, these systems, and this is the point, also block the good ones. Few collective realities are more refractory to the great innovations than VBOs, because the safeguarding of the heritage of the past is a co-essential element in them – unlike companies, there is no change in the "charisma" or "founder" if the market no longer responds: What to change then?

This means, on the level of individuals, that those who happen to have, by destiny and call, a different plumage within the community that generated them – and there are many – must become aware that the resistance, hostility, sometimes persecution and slander that they experience, are largely inevitable, because they are all inscribed in the nature of a VBO. They should learn to live with their own *surplus* and the *misalignments* that each surplus produces, looking after them with meekness.

Community: An experience of returning

At the heart of each person there is a mystery that is revealed, and only in part, throughout their whole life, not seldom in its last part. Even people with many talents, even those who are truly brilliant, find themselves in a state of partial and imperfect knowledge of their own "charisma", their untapped potential, their self-deception and past and present illusions. Therefore, when a person encounters a voice that calls them and their life undergoes a radical turn, if they respond and begin to walk, they do not and cannot know what the development of that encounter will bring, what its fruits, pains and great surprises will be. In a marriage, in an artistic or religious vocation, the wonderful part is the unknown and infinite potential. We do not know what we will become, what the other we tie ourselves to will become, what our relationship will become. What God will become.

Because in every pact and in every promise the most valuable "yes" is not the one said to our present and past and those of the other, but the one pronounced, in the now and reciprocally, to their and our future. That is where the beauty and tragedy of these pacts lie. We live with someone who continually reveals themselves to be different from the person we married; we grow up in a community that is gradually moving away from the one we entered. And day by day as we try to get to know and recognize the person next to us, we also strive to reconcile ourselves with the person we are becoming – and whom we often do not like. The crisis of a relationship is a *plural misalignment* of multiple dimensions where we do not know if it is the novelty of the other or our own that we no longer like – often it is both. Many families keep functioning because human beings have a great resilience to change, especially to the fundamental changes of "you", "I" and "we".

In the spiritual and ideal realm, however, we are generally never sufficiently prepared for the experience (that we sometimes know in the abstract, having read about it in a book) that even the God and/or the ideal we have chosen will change, and it will change a lot, at least as much as we will and, almost always, more than we will. Also, for this reason, the ways, the forms and times in which a response to a vocation develops over time are significantly different, creating a growing diversity.

All organizations have a hard time managing diversity among human beings. Every worker is unique; at any moment they live their own phase in relation to the one that the organization is going through, they cross the many ages of life, suffer traumas and illnesses. However, the organization cannot stay in tune with the life stages of each person, and the show must go on. Theory and practice, however, are showing that various organizational innovations try to *calibrate* employment contracts on the individuals' needs, from young mothers to those who want to earn a degree while working, up to the mature worker who prefers to dedicate more time and energy to their interests and passions, giving up a portion of their salary. Businesses where people live and grow well have understood that workers have different ways of dedicating themselves to the organization, and that the creation of places outside the company where relationships and affectivity can be cultivated improves the overall quality of women and men, also producing a more creative and freer working environment. When, on the other hand, contractual flexibility is low, or when companies use incentives so they don't have to let people free, but capture them with the seduction of money and power, the quality of life worsens inside and outside the company.

In the world of ideal-driven organizations (VBOs), the management of anthropological peculiarities and the life phases of individual members is even more complex, especially for those people who have a strong, identity-shaping relationship with the institution, as happens in religious communities and spiritual movements (but not only in these). A VBO is much more (and, in other ways, much less) than an enterprise. The type of membership, for example, of a Franciscan brother or a Salesian sister in their own community is way too different from a company employment contract, or from the commitment of a volunteer to an association. Personalized contracts do not apply here, nor do incentives increase their "productivity". This discourse is valid not only in the case of people entirely *consecrated* for a cause but whenever the membership in a community or movement is, essentially, a matter of *vocation* – because let us not forget, a vocation is a universal anthropological experience, covering a much wider area than just the religious sphere.

In these cases, belonging to a VBO almost inevitably tends to become an *exclusive* kind of belonging, by choice of the person and the institution. And that is where the more passionate reasoning begins.

A Benedictine brother alternates prayer with work, but when he stops working, he does not really "leave" work to return "home". His return to the community is not like Francesca's, mother of a family, who also leaves the office to return home. They are two substantially different "houses", because while Francesca passes from one sphere of her life (the enterprise) to another (family), governed by distinct principles and sometimes in tension with each other, Father Bernardino actually remains in the same identity-forming environment after he finishes work in the pharmacy of the monastery.

And so if Francesca goes through some difficult moments at work – those moments that we all experience when, for various reasons, enthusiasm for the mission of the enterprise is very low, and we go to work just because we cannot afford not to go there – returning home she meets her children, her friends, then she goes to sing in a choir, she dwells in some places that are very different from her job. In these very different places, Francesca can be *compensated* for the frustrations of the office; she can let off steam, recharge, take refuge; she can walk in gardens enjoying different flowers and air than in the company. This means, *inter alia*, that companies "consume" precious capital that they do not pay for (family, friends, associations etc.), but which make their workers able to work and sometimes even be creative and happy (a sense of taxes can be found here).

Just like Francesca, Father Bernardino has moments when he has no desire to go down and sell herbal teas and spirits; he also experiences being in a bad mood and having conflicts with his colleagues in the shop. But when he returns home, he finds himself living with companions who are very similar (if not identical) to the monks with whom he works. But, and these are the most complex and interesting cases, sometimes Father Bernardino not only does not want to go to the pharmacy; he does not even want to go back to lunch and dinner in the community. He would also need a place where he could get compensated not only for the tensions at work but for the tensions in his community and his whole life. Unlike Francesca, Father Bernardino, however, may not have "compensating spaces" where he can, in a natural and healthy way, take care of the *misalignments* he senses in that specific stage of his life.

Sometimes he manages to stay in church to seek an intimate dialogue with God, who remains a large compensation space when the others have been exhausted, or if they have never existed. But, as we know, in some moments, generally the decisive ones, if you need some air that is different from the only one breathed in inside that community, even the voice of God ends up being enveloped by that same consumed air, and it no longer speaks. In strong charismatic experiences, when one gets misaligned from the community, it is very difficult if not impossible to manage not to also feel a misalignment with God. Crises would be too simple, and therefore not very interesting, if, together with the relationship with the community, the relationship with God that the community has taught us to know, love and recognize were not also in crisis.

The most common and serious crises therefore arise from a syndrome of encirclement because every place is nothing more than a variant of the same single place. And, not infrequently, leaving the community appears to be the only way to be able to breathe again and not die.

In reality, these situations that are so common are the manifestation of something much more radical and important. Adult life inside an identity-creating community, in which we entered in the age of the wonderful providential ignorance of young people, almost always takes *the form of leaving the first community*, even when you remain in exactly the same room and in the same canteen as always.

To understand this statement, which may seem paradoxical or excessive, it is necessary to look carefully at the nature of the relationship between a vocation and the community in which the person is necessarily born, grows and thrives. The community, every community, even of the most free and open type, carries out the function of a *pedagogue* (St. Paul). There comes a day when those who have received a vocation feel the urgent need to greet and thank their pedagogue for finally managing to live as adults, that is, to leave the first community to become something different that neither they themselves nor anyone knows yet. Sometimes you leave by *staying*, at other times you leave by *leaving*. But you always have to leave if you want to return. You can leave for good (even if you stay in the same house) and never come back. But you can also return: Many do and save us every day by coming back to our homes, when perhaps we no longer hope for it.

These departures and these returns generally take the form of *exile*. Exile in Babylon was a decisive stage in the history of salvation; that forced exit from the Holy City of David, the destruction of the only temple of the true God was the time when Israel also made an extraordinary leap in her spiritual experience. The people of Israel understood, in their flesh and without having wished or sought for it, that it is possible to pray to God without the temple, that he remains the true God even if he has become a *defeated God*, that we remain in the community of the covenant even when we leave the promised land. They got to know another great culture and other gods; they were infected by other narratives, also some beautiful ones among them. Without the exile, without that contagion, we now would not have some splendid biblical books, we would not have inherited the lines on the "suffering servant of YHWH". The Bible tells us that it is possible to return from exiles, and that from that *remnant that returns* a child can be born in a manger one day.

You can live well as an adult in the same place of your youth, if community life becomes an experience of returning.

The blessing of the acorns

Throughout their existence, people develop many more dimensions than those useful to the community in which they live and grow up. This is because the "task" we have to perform in the world always exceeds the institutional mission of our organization or community, which remains smaller, however great and extraordinary it may be. No institution is bigger than a single person, because while the collective intelligence of a group or community can solve cognitive problems that are much more complex and richer than those that the individual intelligence can see and think about, the *soul* of a person is increasingly more complex and richer than the "soul" of the community.

Because of this very deep mystery and immense dignity, a person who receives a vocation and sets out on a journey is called to make the whole world a better place, not just that portion of land circumscribed by the confines of his or her community. His or her branches go beyond the garden of the house, spreading spores and seeds that sprout up if they remain free, carried by the wind. When, on the other hand, the community that generates and cares for a vocation wants to become its sole master, and therefore cuts off the branches that go beyond the hedges surrounding the yard, people end up being *consumed* by their community, in objectively incestuous relationships even when everything is animated only by good intentions. The necessary pruning of the branches must not become an *amputation* of someone's vocational profile.

Consumption for internal use is all the more probable if the person is wonderful and full of talent, as it is not easy to understand that this beauty and wealth can live and grow only if given freely and generously. A Franciscan brother comes into the world to make the human family better, not only the Franciscan family, and he will be able to make Franciscanism better if he is left free to do some other things as well. Our *place in the world* does not coincide with the *place* in which we live.

The concrete possibility of leaving is therefore essential for those who depart, but also for those who remain, because the "grandchildren" and the future depend *substantially* on this organizational chastity and generosity (parents who consume their children never become grandparents). This is true in every form of community, even in a cloistered convent, where the experience of taking leave is no less radical since it is often completely interior.

There are many forms of leaving and returning, as many as there are forms that an existential journey may take in each person – infinite, therefore. Sometimes what appears to us and others as a departure (whether physical or spiritual) is actually remaining calm and warm inside the house; at other times it is only after much time that we realize that we left and returned thinking we never moved either in our body or at heart – we were left alone because we were afraid to leave, we had stopped believing in the promise, we had become atheists even though continuing to say the usual prayers. Because life would be too simple and very boring if things responded to the names we give them. They surprise and even floor us, they love to play hide and seek with us. Climbing up on a mountain we hardly ever know if we are coming to Tabor or Golgotha; if there are three tents or three crosses waiting for us on top. It is only as we embrace a cross, ours or that of others, that we discover that that wood releases the same smell as our father's carpentry workshop; and it is there we understand that we worked in that dusty workshop for many years only to recognize the same smell of home in that last smell, that of Joseph and Mary's clothes.

Biblical wisdom gives us some paradigms of departure and return, which trace some anthropological and spiritual coordinates within which some of our concrete experiences can be placed.

A first model is found in the history of Jonah. This prophet receives a call from God to carry out a task, to go and prophesy in the city of Nineveh. But Jonah ran away in the diametrically opposite direction and embarked on a ship to Tarsis. The story does not tell us why Jonah escapes. What interests us is *why* he returns. In fact, while escaping, knowing that he is fleeing his vocation, Jonah has a decisive experience that will bring him back. God unleashes a strong storm on the sea, and the ship is about to sink. Jonah does not notice the storm and sleeps, and then he tells the sailors: "Pick me up and hurl me into the sea... for I know it is because of me that this great tempest has come upon you" (1:12). Jonah feels that the cause of the misfortune that is hitting the ship is *his departure*. He asks to be thrown into the sea, he is saved (thanks to the whale), and he *returns* to his task. It is a tale of stunning human depth, and therefore it is often not understood.

One form of return is that of Jonah. We all leave and run away because at certain times we cannot help but leave, and at a certain point we clearly feel that there is a mysterious but very real relationship between our leaving and the pain of the new people around us. We understand that we are the explanation for the pain of others ("I know", Jonah says). We see a link between the suffering in our enterprise, the misfortune of that family, the illness of this little girl and our running away. We were sleeping on the wrong ship, but one day someone or something wakes us up and when we wake up, we feel with an infallible inner certainty that if we had not embarked on the wrong ship, that pain would not be there. And, sometimes, we are able to return. At other times, we do not go back, because it is too late, or we let ourselves be thrown into the sea and the "whale" does not come to save us. But every now and then, like in Jonah's case, after that return, real miracles happen; our words convert and save entire cities, people and animals. But we did not know it: We only returned to save that ship that was sinking due to our escape.

A second paradigm of departure and return can be found in the story of Joseph in Egypt. Joseph's leave from his family, his father Jacob and his brothers is among the most beautiful and popular biblical stories. The young Joseph was a dreamer and a narrator of dreams. The sharing of these dreams in the community increased his brothers' envy of him, so one day they sold him to merchants making their way to Egypt. Joseph, thanks to his vocation and expertise in the field of dreams, manages to become an important political personality in that foreign land. Years later, during a great famine, when his brothers go to Egypt looking for grain and life, there they find Joseph, the sold brother who will save them.

It is not uncommon that the greatest dreams, those growing beyond the walls of the house are the ones to make us depart, hunt, expel – departures taken from communities are almost never truly voluntary, even when they seem so to us. Those same great and "charismatic" dreams trigger the envy of our brothers. They would like to "kill" our charisma, and sometimes they sell us as slaves. Like Joseph, we do not understand the meaning of all that pain, the reason for all that wickedness on the part of our elder brothers. Then sometimes we arrive in a great kingdom, in a great civilization. Those first unfortunate dreams we made inside the house make us grow and make a career in a foreign land; until one day, without anyone knowing it (neither Joseph nor his brothers), we discover that that painful departure was actually the salvation of all: "So it was not you who sent me here, but God" (Genesis 45:5–8). We take leave to save ourselves, and in the end, we discover that that departure was providence for us and *also* for those who forced us out. It is these paradoxical outcomes that make human life something little "inferior to angels", and it is not rare that the true sense of the score we are playing is only understood in the last note, sometimes during the final applause.

Joseph's departures are above all (but not only) those of youth, when having sincerely tried to follow a voice, after some time you find yourself outside, driven out of the house, into an experience that is lived as deception, betrayal, malice by many, with the anger of having thrown away the best years. But if we ended up in that "cistern" because of honestly following a voice, and if we continue to follow it in the invisible community of our heart even in a foreign land, there almost always comes the moment of salvation, and the rejected stone becomes the corner head of the entire house. It comes much later, but its arrival was inscribed in the good and true logic of life and a mysterious loyalty to a voice that we continued to follow even though we were very confused and disappointed – of these salvations I have known many, and they are among the most sublime human experiences, for every Joseph and his brothers.

Finally, there is an element common to many forms of return after leaving the house. One leaves the house as a son of the community, and then one returns as a father and mother. In these parables of flesh and blood, when the young man who has become an adult in the meantime feels and says, "I will arise and go [back] to my father", when he comes home, the one he finds there to embrace him, throwing his arms around his neck and putting a ring on his finger is no longer his father: *It is his son*. In that departure-return, he became the father of his father, and she became the mother of her mother. But he did not know, he could not know until the moment of the embrace – and, sometimes, he will not know until the very end. In these feasts of return, the fat calf is not killed, because it is *the feast of the blessing of the acorns*, the only food possible and appreciated in the days of distance and poverty, which has now become the food of a new fatherhood.

Mystery is not a profession

Ideal and spiritual communities can hope to become authentic places of human blossoming if they manage to walk on the brink of their own disintegration. When, on the other hand, the fear of the possibility of one's own end becomes too strong and prevails, the life of the members withers due to a serious lack of air and sky. Only the ridges of the high altitudes allow the view of landscapes that are wide enough to (almost) satisfy the desire for infinity that pushes people with a "vocation" to offer their lives to communities to which they entrust essential pieces of their freedom and interiority. But as soon as the caravan loses altitude in search of safe bivouacs where to fix the tents, the places and horizons immediately become too narrow: We just have to dismantle the camp quickly and resume climbing. On the ridges there is a risk of slipping and falling, but it's only from there that you can touch the sky. Many communities have become extinct simply because they tried to make their people really live (and, sometimes, a sprout reappears rising again from the broken trunk); others have survived because they have never begun to live a daring and full life. Christianity was born out of the disintegration of its first community. Jesus saved his own because he did not "save" them by bringing them to safe and well-guarded places. He slipped into the underworld, and it was from there, to the amazement of all, that he began his resurrection.

In ideal-driven communities something similar happens to what we live with our sons and daughters. In the morning we secretly watch them put their ties or blouses on in front of the mirror. We are proud of their beauty and goodness, and happy to let them go, and they never cease to amaze us when we see them return every night. Because we know that one day they will not come back, but if we really let them go, we can hope that in another day they really will. Families and communities die when the fear of the possible non-return of those close to us takes away the joy of seeing them leave in the morning, reducing the pride felt about their beauty to the point of perverting it in jealousy. To try to stay in the high and luminous trajectories, a decisive operation is the custody of the difference between the ideal community and the ideal of the community. In other words, everything should be done so that the person who arrives because of a call does not identify the ideals that attract them and seduce them with the community itself and with its practices. However, it is all too common for VBOs to present themselves as the perfect incarnation of the ideals that inspire and animate them. That's because the temptation of the community to present itself to its members as the ideal to live and follow is too strong. Also because the ideal-community identification is very much appreciated by both people and the community, especially in the early stages – but it is at the very beginning that we should act in a persistent direction and contrary to the "natural" one.

So it happens that instead of marking and maintaining the surplus of the ideal of the community over its practices, the VBOs *operationalize* their "charisma" in a set of actions, rites, liturgies, individual and collective rules. We are all convinced, and all of us in good faith, that the rules, regulations and practices are the perfect certified copy of the ideal; that the way, the only sure way to make the encounter with the voice calling us yesterday concrete today is to follow those rules and practices, *sine glossa*. The founders and communities make this perfect translation because they believe that without the *operationalization* of ideals their community will have no future. They gradually eliminate the surplus of the ideal over the community, and so without wanting or knowing it, they actually prevent the charisma from continuing to work new things in the future, because novelty flourishes only from the wounds/embrasures of the surplus-discards between ideals and their historical translation – the unintended effects are always the decisive ones in collective experiences. When this surplus is gone, the free and infinite spirit becomes a technique. The "what is it?" – namely an exclamation of the heart that comes every time we come across the manna (*man hu*: What is it?) in the desert of a spiritual event of salvation – becomes: "How does it work?", "how do I realise it?", "how do I put it into practice?". The first encounter that generated the desire to know who and what that marvellous voice was progressively turns into a repertoire of good practices and rules to follow in order to remain "faithful", because communities cannot be born without some translation of the charisma into practice, but this translation itself risks silencing the charisma that generated them – a paradoxical tension, which is vital and always decisive.

All this is very well known to biblical humanism. The Bible has done almost everything possible to distinguish YHWH from the Law and the word of the prophets who spoke in his name (without always succeeding). But if the Bible had lost this overflow of God over its words, it would have used the word as a string to trap God, reducing him to an idol (every idolatry, even the "secular" ones, is a double string: Men who bind the divinity and the divinity that, once transformed into an idol, binds its worshippers-glamorizers). The words of scripture can generate other true words because they are the sacrament of a reality the mystery of which they do not know. Biblical humanism has succeeded in saving this surplus thanks to the prophets. Similarly to them, the founders of charismatic communities are called to be the first guardians of the surplus of the charism over the words of the charism. But when ideals come to coincide with the whole of the community practices, the free interior space is progressively reduced in individuals. And the first desire to know what and who the mystery we had encountered was gradually becomes a simple profession.

All this has very concrete and sometimes dramatic existential consequences. Many members of VBOs go into deep crisis when they realize that although they are surrounded by practices and words that only and always talk about spirituality and ideality, as a matter of fact, they no longer know what inner life and spirituality really are. Moreover, it is not uncommon for people who started out in them as youth with a great thirst for spirituality to discover themselves impoverished as adults – in precisely what should have represented their distinctive trait and the ideal of their lives. They can no longer say true and wise words to anyone, not even to themselves. When someone meets them, they find themselves in front of a profession, of technical answers without the specific competence in the spirit that only the practice of freedom can generate in an inhabited heart. They find that what they possess is an ideal that has become ethical and practical, that no longer speaks of spirituality, or life or God. The cancellation of surpluses between the God of the community and the community because it was presented as the perfect incarnation of that God cancelled the inner and most secret space where the inner life is cultivated and nourished. And after talking about spirituality for many years, they suddenly find themselves in a neo-atheistic condition. They feel that they have only used techniques; they have remained on the surface of true inner life for a lack of freedom and breath. Because once the words of the community are extinguished, they can no longer speak to God, or of God or to their own hearts – a dramatic discovery, which often produces infinite anger and pain, but which can sometimes become a great blessing if a resurrection begins in that hell. Still others, and these are the saddest and most common cases, continue to live until the end, identifying themselves with the profession without ever realizing that they have lost contact with the spirituality that once attracted them.

Communities live and make people live well if they help their people never to lose the dialogue about "who are you?"; if they leave them free spaces for the soul and life to fill (never completely) with personalized dialogues that feed the questions and reduce the simple and equal answers for all. Because the real voices calling us know only the "you" of the second person singular: Collective nouns do not work for these very serious things. They only work if they free themselves from the practices and the Law to allow everyone the freedom to know and follow the spirit that speaks to everyone in a different language. Community practices are only good if they coexist with individual ones, born of different words whispered by the same ideal, every day, to everyone, in an essential biodiversity. But all this is extremely dangerous and therefore very rare. Always there is the fear that the best people and the ones most attracted by the peaks slip from the ridge; that they become so free that they do not come back home in the evening, that they sleep in mountain huts to venture on new solitary climbs of the mountains of youth at dawn. And so, almost always, communities fill all inner spaces, they crowd the landscape and find themselves with people who are less alive and fruitful but safer and more aligned – who feel great as young people, but bad as adults and old people.

These processes are mostly inevitable and tend to happen in every community's life. Including families, where after the early days of falling in love dominated by "who are you?", we soon move on to "how does it work?" But, as we know very well, families don't work anymore if the questions do not come back every now and then: "Who are you?", "Who am I?", "What have we become?". Moses, the man who spoke to YHWH "mouth to mouth", never saw the face of God. He knew and recognized his voice, but not his face. Once, once only, at the height of a wonderful dialogue with the voice, Moses asked for the impossible: "Show me your glory!". YHWH answered him, "I will cover you with my hand until I have passed by. Then I will take away my hand, and you shall see my back, but my face shall not be seen" (33:21–3). Communities must learn to be docile under the hand of their own ideals covering their eyes, to be content with the naked voice, to know that in those very rare times when the hand is removed, they can only see the back. The practices, the rules, the objects of the community "cult" are only copies of the back of the ideal seen in some very special moment of light. But the face, the intimacy and the light of the eyes remain and must remain mystery and desire, and, above all, must not be confused with the back. When Mary Magdalene, in tears, met the Risen One, she did not recognize his face: She recognized a voice calling her by name.

Truth is not in success

The first and most precious dowry that those who join in a community bring with them is the experience of the voice that called them. The nature of this wonderful dialogue, made up of a few words and a lot of body, is the spiritual *fingerprint* of the person. It is formed in the "mother's womb" and then does not change for the rest of one's life. Even if there are wounds, the skin grows again with the same unique and unrepeatable characteristics. And it is not unusual that when we meet a person at the time of their first vocational encounter and then again after decades: although they have changed a lot, before recognizing them in their changed somatic traits, we recognize them from the spiritual imprint that has remained in them beyond the events transforming their body and soul. Indeed, we can become very different, sometimes even very ugly, but that imprint is there, it will be there in us until the end, and even if we decide to cancel it or remove it through surgery, it remains tenaciously, waiting for us faithfully, being more faithful than us.

True vocations are never abstract: "Go to the land that *I will show you*"; "Go and free my people *enslaved in Egypt*". There is nothing more concrete than a vocation – and when it is abstract, it is almost never authentic. Your calling is not to art in general, but to poetry – you are an artist because you are a poet, not vice versa. Your calling is not to become a nun, but to become a Salesian sister – even if sometimes it takes some time to understand it.

In vocations, in all true vocations, *everything* is in the voice. It is an *auditory* event. There is a real, mysterious and very concrete experience of a voice that calls and speaks to us and asks us to do something. A vocation lies in this dialogue between voices: The one that calls and the one that responds to it or that of the community that welcomes it. There is almost never certainty about *who* is calling, only about the presence of a voice. It is a plural voice that never calls us to become *just one thing*. It calls amidst life's ordinary conditions, with all its beauties, contradictions and wounds. Some who marry are no less fascinated by mysticism and spirituality than some cloistered nuns. Those whom the voice asks to be a celibate do not have a different psychological structure than those who marry. They have, on average, the same desires, the same passions, the same *eros* of all. They were not called *because* they had an anthropological predisposition for chastity or obedience: *They were called and that is it*, without prior motivational and aptitude interviews. And it is not true that the voice that calls also provides the means to be able to carry out the task that it asks for. It would be too simple, and therefore trivial and not true – these things happen when it comes to company assignments, but not when carrying out our assignment for the world. *Inadequacy* is the ordinary condition of every vocation, and perhaps of every honest person.

Thus, among those who have received an authentic vocation, there are some balanced and some neurotic people, there are healthy and sick, holy and sinful ones: Generally, they are not any wiser or more intelligent than the average population. Sometimes the honest response to a vocation makes people acquire some virtues over time and people improve ethically, at other times not. These calls coexist with and within chronic illnesses, depressions, accidents, wounds, and some people remain nailed to crosses on an eternal Good Friday and await a resurrection that does not come at all. In the best communities there are some people who are brought to spirituality and others who are not, some who love long prayers, some who do not love them at all. Others who started with great religious needs and after decades found themselves with a vocation that became a civil commitment among the poor; while learning to listen to the voices of the victims they forgot the timbre of the first voice – to discover at the end that the voice of the first meeting has got lost, because it turned into the voice of the pain of others.

This biodiversity of the population of communities raises important, sometimes decisive, questions about the processes of *selection* and *discernment*.

The only authentic and essential discernment that would serve at the dawn of a call is to ascertain the *presence of the voice* that is calling, which tends to be confused with other voices that, at a young age, are very similar to it. But the "masters" capable of these discoveries are very rare, today more than yesterday. And so, in the inability to find the only true indicator of the authenticity of a vocation, some secondary criteria are used to capture secondary and accidental aspects, but not the vocation. This inauspicious outcome depends entirely on the – nowadays deeply rooted – idea that the *pre-conditions of the call* must be sought in people. We tend to seek (in the context of consecrated life, for example) presumed predispositions for chastity, for community life, or perhaps for obedience. As if we could identify an abstract attitude for community *before really living* in a concrete community, or for chastity forgetting that the experience of chastity at 40 or 50 years old is radically different from the one *imagined* at 20, in the age of enchantment.

Vocations are always "experience goods", that is, goods whose true value can only be known after they have been "consumed". We begin a journey with the *idea of vocation*, and until we are inside a vocational experience, we know almost nothing about our concrete vocation. That is why every true vocational experience is tragic, because it carries the possibility of its failure within itself. Among those who leave an ideal-driven community there are not only those who have been "wrong about their vocation"; there are also many who initially had a true call, but in the *experience* they have gone through they have understood that they could not live in the concrete condition in which that call placed them existentially – because of their own weaknesses or because of community neuroses and errors of government. Therefore, the failure of a concrete vocational experience does not say much about the presence or absence of a true call at the beginning. There are people who remain, feeling very well within a vocational experience for the whole of their lives without ever having had a vocation, and others who leave even though they had a true call that accompanies them throughout their lives, just as there are communities saved by reformers who had lousy attitudes and great weaknesses but had simply been called.

However, if in order to prevent failures (a noble and dutiful intention) we try to identify the psychological or character-related predispositions of the people who have been called, and we neglect to understand if at the beginning there was a true vocational experience, we prevent people with weaknesses but a calling from being able to occupy their place in the world, even when this place is at stake, because of those weaknesses, from being uncomfortable and painful, even from having to deal with failure. Because no one can know, either before or after the event, the spiritual and moral value of a year, ten or 30 years lived trying to be faithful to a true call, even when that experience was interrupted, sometimes by the errors and wickedness of those around and above us. Something very similar happens in every marriage experience: If there was a real call at the beginning, the love we felt for each other, the children we gave birth to remain a blessing even if we have not been able to live together forever. At the same time, there are also some existences lived without traumas and failures the reason for which may be that we followed only the incentives and interests, and at the beginning of these there was no real voice. Success is not the indicator of the truth of an existence – even here the prophets are our eternal and infinite masters. It is the truth of what we are living and what we have lived that says the value of an experience and a life.

We must not make the cognitive error of "peak-end effects" in the evaluation of our existential experiences. We make these mistakes when, for example, we listen to a symphony with the old vinyl, and after an hour of listening to Beethoven, towards the end, the record is damaged and starts to make ugly and annoying sounds. Generally, when we evaluate that experience, we forget the hour of heavenly music and extend the last-minute nuisance (the end) to the whole listening experience, expressing a negative opinion on the whole event. As a matter of fact, we had a wonderful hour and a strenuous ending. The beauty and truth of years spent kindly following a real voice are not to be measured by the unhappy final "minute", by the damaged record or by the old, broken record player. No one can and must ruin the truth and the beauty of having spent that first hour in Beethoven's company.

When, on the other hand, we look for vocational signs in character and personality, we end up identifying *predisposed* people who, however, are almost never those called by a real voice, but attracted by the *sociological aspects of the vocational profession*. Because if to enter communities it is the people who love community life very much and/or do not have the same affective desires as everyone else, have less eros and human passions than others, then we end up with communities poor in terms of anthropological normality, having little biodiversity and generativity. In such communities, people are too similar and have a "reduced humanity" because they have already entered similar and reduced – but life is generous, and even if we entered a community with the wrong motivations, we can always receive a true call until the last day, provided that we really wish to be called by name on the day before.

In ideal-driven communities we are *together* because *each one of us* is called. One does not enter because we like the notion of we, but because we say yes to a *you*. In Galilee no community was created because the apostles were attracted by some form of common life or a state of life – and we don't know if Peter or Judas was the one more sociologically and psychologically *predisposed* for community life. The most lively and true community experiences almost always happen among people who would not have the ideal character traits to live together, but it is there, among them that an authentic, improbable fraternity flourishes, which has the capacity to convert and generate. Communities formed by people who are all equally attracted to the community itself often become communities that attract no one – communities with little biodiversity do not go beyond the second generation.

Many painters did not know painting techniques the day they received their vocation. They learned the techniques later, but they were *already* artists. You can *learn* community life, you can even learn to live in poverty and chastity, but you cannot learn a vocation. You can only listen to it and then start the journey.

The demolition of the idol

Those who have made faith – any faith, not just religious faith – the foundation of their lives, those who have made it the existential theme of their life and not one theme of the many, live constantly in fear of having founded their lives on deception, of having built an admirable building on nothing. For a long time, this fear remains latent, especially when we are young: It appears from time to time and then waves us good-bye to let us live the time of enchantment in full, which is necessary to make our crazy flights possible. But, under the surface, it grows together with faith. Until, in an adult stage of existence, it emerges and imposes itself with an invincible force. It surprises us, it bothers us a lot and it does not let us sleep.

We suddenly realize that that fear was well founded, and the possibility of nothingness becomes a real experience. We had deceived ourselves, *effectively*. It is the experience of the lack of foundation, total misalignment, the *bewilderment* of the exile. We find ourselves in a completely new land, as inhabitants of the empire that we feared and hated for so many years. At first, we try to orient ourselves in the new landscape; we look for the signs of the landscape of the country where we grew up. We look for the tower, the bell tower, the clock in the ways in which we have always known them. We don't find them, and *we get lost*. They are actually even there, but we cannot see them.

In other words, we realize that we had not believed in God but in an idol. And it is here that the spiritual journey must become an experience of *demolition*. On the day of his call, the voice reveals to the prophet Jeremiah his mission and destiny: "I have set you this day over nations and over kingdoms, / to pluck up and to break down, / to destroy and to overthrow, / to build and to plant" (1:4–10). In the beginning there is planting and building. The knocking down phase, when it comes, comes later.

The most important reality that is destroyed during a vocational journey is the *idea of God* and the *ideal*. Before being a destruction of the "I", a vocation is a destruction of God, a demolition of the image that we have made of him and in which we believe. The Bible has placed as its first commandment the prohibition of making images of God because *every image of God is an idol*. But already from the day after that of our vocation, we all construct our own image of God, and *therefore* our idol. We are not aware of it, so we are innocent. Destruction is therefore essential to be able to leave the age of idolatry – in the Bible the destruction of the temple and exile made it possible for that different faith not to become idolatry.

Here lies, perhaps, one of the many meanings of that mysterious and paradoxical phrase (*koan*) of the Zen tradition: "If you meet a Buddha on the street, kill him". The "Buddha" along the adult stretch of the road is not only the teacher who made us discover the spiritual path. It is also the idea-image of God that that master or community had given us at the beginning.

This demolition takes various forms. Sometimes that first image disappears little by little like a statue consumed by the wind and the rain (which we continually try to restore, however). At other times, it is an earthquake in our land that makes it implode, and it is not uncommon for us to remain under the rubble. Sometimes, and these are the most interesting but difficult to understand and say, *it is we* who take the pickaxe and start to hit that statue, because we understand that it was an idol that, like all idols, was devouring us day after day. Because we realize that if we do not destroy our statue of God, it will destroy us. Faiths are authentic places of liberation if one day they become experiences of destruction.

When this process happens in a community, a spiritual movement or a VBO, the community also gets involved in the destruction. If we learned the first idea of the ideal from the community that gave it concreteness and words, the need to destroy the statue of God inevitably becomes also the *demolition of the community* that had given and taught it to us. Together with the image of God, the image of the community that guarded it – its practices, faces and prayers – also disappears. We demolish it because it has the same idolatrous signs. This destruction – which never remains entirely intimate, and is expressed in public criticism, sarcasm, in judgements towards everything and everyone – also contains some hidden but precious messages for that community, because it tells it about the vital need it has for self-subversion. But in every community there is the terror of its own destruction, because it is very difficult for it to understand that if it does not destroy the idol of the ideal it has built, it is condemned to death – and so along with all of itself it preserves the idol confused with the ideal.

The decisive element that often prevents the beginning of demolition works is the absolute lack of guarantee that a new faith will take the place of what we should and would like to demolish. It is the terror of losing God forever along with the image we had of him that leads many people who had received an authentic spiritual call not to destroy the idol and to remain forever in the idolatrous stage of faith (we like idols very much because they do not ask us to take any risks).

For many, this stage of the God of the call becoming the idol of adult life takes place in perfect, absolute and innocent *good faith*. For others, instead, it takes the form of what Sartre calls *bad faith* (a word that he uses in a different sense from the common one): They renounce exercising the radical risk of freedom, and thus remain stuck in a sort of moral limbo, where they are both believers and idolaters, faithful and atheists, true and false. Those in good faith are on a theatre stage to recite a comedy-tragedy, but they are convinced that the stage is life; the ones in bad faith know that they are reciting a script that is not life, but they do not want to go off the stage anymore because elsewhere they would be attacked and destroyed by *anxiety*. But those who manage to overcome bad faith (or at least to recognize it and decide to want to overcome it) and then carry out this demolition of the idol of God, find themselves within one of the highest and most extraordinary human experiences. They precipitate in a condition very similar, if not identical, to that of atheists. They perceive – see and feel – nothingness underlying all things, a *vanitas* that with its dense smoke envelops the full interior and exterior landscape. But, unlike those who do not believe because they have never believed, when the experience of this nothing comes after a true life of faith, the confrontation with this desolate land is almost always devastating.

In reality, the radical experience of the absence of God is ethically preferable to idolatry, because the nothing that comes as the maturation of faith is an evolutionary, spiritual and anthropological leap, but the person who finds themselves within the experience does not perceive any evolution, only an infinite solitude in a world without gods. The same disorientation is almost always experienced by those who observe and accompany those who live these experiences. Hence, they are the first ones to be afraid facing the first blows, and then do everything to remove the pickaxe from our hands.

Then there are some typical challenges that are little explored, though crucial – it is not easy to explore these abysses of life. When this demolition phase takes place within a community, the inner exile is joined by the outer exile. You live with fellow citizens who go through different stages of life, some in good faith, others in bad faith, and you feel totally strangers in your own house. Also because in communities there are very few people who remain after the demolition. Many of those interrupting an authentic community journey are those who feel exhausted at the end of the demolition – perhaps because that first statue was too imposing and robust – and have not found the resources to continue. For these demolishers of idols, life becomes very hard in communities. The discussions around the table, the liturgies and the many activities that they continue do not only become uninteresting but also cause new pain to them. One remains in one's job, as always, in a destitution of answers and light, in which one remains for years, even decades. It is very likely that when we hear different and truer words about life and spirit from someone, this person is in this phase of life – but they do not tell us, they would not know how to tell us, because words cannot be found for that (going through and telling about what you have lived through are two different "skills", especially at certain times in life).

But if we manage to get to the bottom of this demolition, a splendid stage of life can begin, the most beautiful and true of all. We truly become a brother or sister to all men and women, rediscovering the same integral human condition that precedes faith and non-faith. We become beggars of meaning towards all those we meet, in the street, in books, in poetry. We go back to being a child and ask everyone: "Why?", and a new ignorant and enchanted kind of listening is born. We esteem all those who, without having the faith that we had, manage to work, bring children into the world or die without despair and love. And our anger becomes strong because we do not succeed. We come to curse that image that has prevented us from learning the job of living, because we discover ourselves much less skilled in this fundamental art than "normal" women and men are. But if you still want to read the Bible, you finally begin to understand a few pages of Job, Isaiah, some of the psalms which remained unknown to us or bothered us before. Without the experience of destruction much of the Bible and life remain inaccessible. And we begin to give thanks for this new epiphany of life and word.

After a life spent in an environment populated by God, the disappearance of the sacred frees our sight to begin to see man, finally. The place cleared of religion becomes a kind of humanism. By chasing away the money changers from the temple, the doves and goats from its altars, the Earth was freed to welcome a different kingdom. Sometimes, after the destruction, a new faith and a new community of faith returns – which will then leave us again, to take us back to other exiles where we will become even more human. Sometimes prayer blooms again, crying out for the pain of men and women. At other times faith does not return. We enter the church not to pray but to hope that it will come back and surprise us from behind while we are sitting in the pews watching an empty tabernacle. But we do not regret having destroyed the fetish, and we would not go back for anything in the world. The job of living is what remains. The same expectation of God is what remains.

The tree of our children is more beautiful

Family, work and school are all matters of reciprocity. The care we give remains imperfect unless we sometimes experience being assisted by those we assist, and no education is effective if while doing his lesson the teacher does not learn and change with his students. The relationship between ideal-driven communities and the people who are part of them is also a matter of reciprocity, which lives on a great *closeness* combined with a real *distance*. Nothing on Earth is more intimate than an encounter in the spirit between people called to the same destiny by the same voice. That is when we see the very desires of our heart in the other, when our said and not said words come back to us multiplied and sublimated. We rejoice in the same things, and the joy increases in seeing that the other is rejoicing for the same reasons and in the same way that we are.

This *mutual indwelling* ("wert thou known / To me, as thoroughly I to thee am known": Dante, *Paradise*; English translation by the Rev. H.F. Cary, MA) is, however, a fully human and humanizing experience if it coexists with respect for a form of *distance*, which protects against the temptation to possess the other, to appropriate that *overflow* which is in its mystery. It is mainly inside this free and saved space that communion lives and feeds itself, which however grows and makes it grow until we leave the other and our heart free to veil a "not yet" that can be revealed tomorrow but only in part.

This dynamic of closeness and distance, already difficult between individuals, is even more demanding in the relationships between the individual and their community. Here, it can happen that communion between the personal and community spirits turns into an activity of *substitution*. Those who arrive in an ideal-driven community are fascinated and submerged by the beauty and spiritual richness they encounter there, which is much more sparkling and seductive than the little voice inside them. In fact, it appears less interesting and luminous than what they find around and outside themselves. That little dowry with which they knock on the doors of the community does not shine and cannot shine, because it is neither a pearl nor a diamond: It is, simply, a *seed*. But it is precisely in that tiny thing that the possibility of a good future, real innovations, surprises, reform, great trees and new fruits lies, both for the person and the community.

Therefore, those responsible should do everything possible to keep that unique and special intimacy in the person alive and fruitful, which *precedes* the encounter with the charism of the community. And so to dose the transmission of the spiritual heritage and collective ideal very well, with the necessary care and chastity so as not to submerge and suffocate that small primeval seed.

The *principle of subsidiarity*, a pillar of Christian and European human-ism, also applies to the management of the individual-community relation-ship: What comes from the exterior, from above and from outside, is good if it helps what is intimate, close and personal (as a *subsidy*, or support). Much of the quality and maintenance of a vocational history depends on the sub-sidiary dialogue between these two *intimacies*, especially in the early days; on the capacity not to replace the first intimacy (which is small, naive and simple) with the second (which is great, mature and spectacular). Because that place where a free, attentive, cultivated, critical thought lives and grows is the first intimacy, because it draws on deeper layers than those nourishing the common charisma. It draws water directly from the spiritual tradition that nourishes the same community charisma, and from the traditions of the human civilizations, founding both. It is nourished by the prayers of all, not only by our prayers but the poems, novels and art of all humanity, by the love and pain of every human being and the Earth.

But it is almost impossible that this substitution between the two intima-cies does not take place, as it is sought and desired by the individual person, in the first place. The person is deeply fascinated by the new great words they find upon arriving, also because they notice that what comes to them from outside was *already present* within them, and that they are strength-ened and exalted in the charismatic community. They know intimately what is given them from outside because while they receive it, they recognize it as something that was already intimately present in them. However, when we treat that young woman as if she were coming as a spiritual *tabula rasa* in Franciscan matters, all we do is we kill that first intimacy in her that already contained essential chromosomes to make herself and *her commu-nity* become authentically Franciscan. Authentic spiritual paths do not *begin* but *continue* in a community, because they had already begun outside, in a first intimacy.

After Saul's encounter with the Lord on the road to Damascus, he arrived at Ananias' house who baptized him, and he received the Christian faith from that community. But Paul always remembered and claimed that his vocation had been earlier than his meeting with Ananias, and that voice continued to nourish him together with the one that spoke to him in his community, and every now and then it told him words he did not under-stand: "the gospel... I did not receive it from any man, nor was I taught it, but I received it through a revelation of Jesus Christ" (Galatians 1:11–2). In the communities the main mechanism of spiritual discernment starts from the intimacy of the person and is accomplished in the collective intimacy that becomes the final exegete of individual words. But the reverse process is also essential, when we return to the dialogue of the first intimacy to decipher the collective words that we do not understand, and that – once understood inside and given back outside – enrich everyone. When this second move is missing, the members of the community tend to become all too similar to each other, because the place of anthropological and spiritual biodiversity, and therefore of the richness and generativity of charisms is not the second intimacy, but the *first*.

When human babies are born, they are very similar and all seem the same in their first days, and only by growing up do they become different and assume their specific features. In spiritual births, however, the opposite happens: At the beginning, we are all very different, each with a unique colour of eyes and hair; then, once we enter a community, over time we tend to become spiritually more and more similar, because the second, collective vocational intimacy grows at the expense of the first. And the intoxicating fusion of the first years gives way to common and equal words that speak less and less.

Spiritual and prophetic communities always struggle to recognize the value of the first intimacy because of the great esteem and consideration they have (and must have) for the second collective spiritual intimacy. Often they see it as the only one necessary, which incorporates and understands the first and is considered as the milk teeth of children, which must fall out in order to let the adult and permanent teeth emerge. And so they often determine, in good faith, the progressive atrophy of the first vocational place that also sustains the second one – much damage is produced by much good faith, which however does not cancel out the consequences or a lot of pain.

The more it is true for a community that it has a strong prophetic and charismatic dimension, the more naturally and spontaneously it underestimates spiritual experiences prior to arrival. This way they are forgetting that every organization, even the most genuinely charismatic one, has a continuous need for self-regeneration, and the first instrument of this is the prophecy of its people, which however must be recognized and given the space to be cultivated. Also the people of Israel needed to be accompanied by giant prophets for centuries, even though they were already a holy and prophetic nation. Without the prophets who have continually renewed it (and that the people continued to kill) even that different community would have turned into a religious monolith without the spirit. And what would the Church have become without thousands of prophets and saints who have brought it back to its vocation and conversion a thousand times? So it happens also for every community, which is already charismatic by vocation: The providential arrival of prophets *who guard the two intimacies* saves it and converts it every day.

The replacement of the first with the second intimacy is also the root of much malaise in ideal and spiritual communities. The repetition and reiteration of the same collective intimacy for years, which is no longer accompanied and nourished by that first deep intimate dialogue generates progressive and radical identity diseases in people. The great energy invested in learning the art of answering questions about "who are we?" progressively consumes the ability to answer the other radical question: "And me, who am I?" Anyone who knows the essentials of the spiritual universe knows well that "who am I?" is a question that has no satisfactory answer. But there is a good and a bad way of not answering this question. The first comes from the awareness that the answer changes and grows with us, and that perhaps only the angel of death will reveal it to us as he embraces us. The bad way, on the other hand, is the no-response that comes from going deep inside the heart and finding only attempts to answer it, composed with the collective words declined in the first-person plural. The constant and continuous exercise of conjugation of the verbs of life in the plural has consumed the very possibility of a logos in the singular; we do not answer "no" because the question has no convincing answers, but because we have forgotten the grammatical and syntactical rules to *understand* the question.

However, when we manage to preserve that first intimacy (and, thanks be to God, it often happens) and defend it with all our strength from ourselves and from our community, we find a great treasure in adult life. It becomes the essential good when the second intimacy of the community withdraws – and it must withdraw – taking away with it the words, images and symbols with which we had embellished our spiritual life and our entire world. There we realize that in that land *there was still a tree*. We embrace it, we feed on its fruits and we enjoy its shadow. And then we discover, moved, that it is the same "tree of life" that we had seen in the Eden of the first paradise, because it grew from the tenacious custody of one of its true seeds. Under that single shadow old and new companions begin to gather, and a new story begins again.

If on the day of the great withdrawal of the waters in our land, we do not find any trees, we can set out in desperate search of a good seed and entrust it to that fertile land. It will not be our tree; it will be our children's – and perhaps that is even more beautiful.

Conclusion

This small book is a preliminary analysis of values-based organizations (VBOs), carried out "in prose" and in a language accessible even to non-specialists in economics or organization theory. Once we entered this territory, still almost entirely virgin for economic and social sciences, we did not write on the map, as the ancient explorers of the African continent, *hic sunt leones*, did. We tried instead to explore some areas of the region. Walking and drawing some first coordinates, we found ourselves almost suddenly in a very luxuriant and splendid region, full of colours, rare flowers, cascades of living water. A real forest, which seemed mysterious and fascinating to look at from the outside, described and sung about for its beauty by poets, theologians and saints; but there were no maps to try to learn about the inside of that wonderful and very fertile forest, abundant in animals, birds, life and an extraordinary biodiversity. There were only travellers' stories, some sketches of some ravines encountered by more than one explorer and many legends. However, there was no description of the paths, dangers, cultures and traditions of the human communities within it, its typical illnesses and its care. It was the land of "charismatic" communities and organizations. In fact, on this forest and its inhabitants, some stories and descriptions were found scattered, but they lacked in decisive aspects to know the nature and the morphology of this beautiful territory. There was a "secular" and sufficiently thorough analysis of the typical organizational illnesses of charismatic realities, of the risks hidden behind the management of the people who received a vocation, and of many other things.

Among the many possible perspectives of a work dedicated to the issue of values-based organizations, we have decided to pay special attention to the moments of transition or those of crisis of both people and organizations, especially the complex and problematic ones that concern identity, which is crucial for the development of every type of organization and not only VBOs. When it works out and flourishes, individual and collective life can be seen as a sequence of crises that have been faced and overcome.

And each crisis is ambivalent. It could be the beginning of a new spring, it could create the right conditions so we can find our profound vocation, but it could also make us worse and block the way to our psychological and spiritual growth. This is one more reason why we should give importance to examining the nature of relationships that occur inside such organizations in order to understand better their morphology and intervene with more effective instruments in the moments when the crisis occurs – this is crucial: Almost always the starting point of a vital process is the most important one – and manage to overcome them successfully.

At the end of this analysis, maybe the idea to write a book on VBOs is less odd. Religious organizations, social economy and non-profit organizations have shown down through the centuries that there has always been, and there still is, a place in the economic field for some things other than profit maximization. Those who want to tell economic history correctly, know that, in the past as in the present, in the economic domain right next to the biggest sins stand also big virtues, people who have rendered and continue to render it a place of authentic human and spiritual excellence. But when the ideals penetrate the economic and civil field, the human relationships make them at once more complex and richer: The conflicts, the risks and the mistakes increase but the same also happens with the quality of life, inside and outside of the organizations. The "wounds" arise but, along with them, also come the "blessings", and it is often impossible to separate them (Bruni 2012). This book is a contribution to understanding the bigger complexity of organizations when ideals are taken seriously.

Finally, surpluses and misalignments are the ordinary and constant condition of VBOs. Like all complex realities, these too constantly live on the verge of their possibilities. The people whom they welcome and who in turn enrich them are constantly evolving. They fall asleep having reached a certain balance in the contradictions, joys and sorrows of that day, and when they wake up, they have to start looking for another one again. As young people they want paradise, as adults they find themselves in many purgatories and in some hell, too, until as old people they realize that they have never left that first paradise – but to understand it they needed a lifetime, and a little more. But also communities and organizations continually create and undo their balances, and when they don't, they start to die. The life of those who take ideals seriously (and are many, more than we think) is a play that takes place between people who produce surplus and are misaligned and who live and change within collective realities that are also changing and that displace them every day. The ability to live in *unbalance* is therefore the first art that people and organizations must learn. They should learn to walk on the wire, like the equilibrist who does not fall as long as he continues to move. It is an uncomfortable condition, but the only vital one because it is capable of generating real novelties. Then, once we get to the other end of the wire, another crossing over another abyss awaits us; until the end, when we discover that by the force of moving our arms not to fall, we have actually learned to fly.

When in the night something or someone wakes us up, some do not open their eyes and try to fall asleep again reconnecting with the dream they were having, and so they can resume their sleep and dreams. But there are other people who, if interrupted in their sleep, open their eyes, turn on the light, read a novel, begin to pray, open the window and then watch the dawn. In this series of *surpluses* and *misalignments*, we have sensed that when something or a cry of pain wakes us up in the middle of the first great dream of youth, we don't have to keep our eyes closed to return to the first, interrupted dream. That waking up is the time for a new dawn, for another sun that awaits us beyond the closed shutter. It is the time for the new sounds and colours of the new day; it is the time for the different and no less great dreams of adult life – adult life of people, adult life of organizations.

Bibliography

Antoci A., Bruni L., Russu P., Smerilli A., The Founder's Curse: The Stronger the Founder, the Weaker the Organization, *Communications in Nonlinear Science and Numerical Simulation*, 2020, vol. 84, art. no. 105190.

Benjamin W., Capitalism as Religion (1921), Translated into English by Chad Kautzer from the *Gesammelte Schriften*, Volume VI, ed. Ralph Liedemann and Hermann, Schweppenhäuser, Suhrkamp Verlag, Frankfurt, 1985.

Bruni L., Smerilli A., *Benedetta economia*, Città Nuova, Roma, 2008.

Bruni L., Smerilli A., The Value of Vocation. The Crucial Role of Intrinsically Motivated People in Values-Based Organizations, in *Review of Social Economy*, 2009, vol. 67, 3, pp. 271–288.

Bruni L., *The Wound and the Blessing*. Newcity, New York, 2012.

Bruni L., Sena B. (ed.), *The Charismatic Principle in Economic and Social Life*, Routledge, London, 2012.

Bruni L., Smerilli A., *L'altra metà dell'economia*, Città Nuova, Roma, 2014.

Bruni L., *La distruzione creatrice. L'arte della gestione delle crisi nelle Organizzazione a Movente Ideale*, Città Nuova, Roma, 2015.

Bruni L., Smerilli A., *The Economics of Value-Based-Organisations. An Introduction*, Routledge, London, 2015.

Bruni L., *The Economy of Salvation. Ethical and Anthropological Foundations of Market Relations in the First Two Books of the Bible*, vol. 4, Springer, Cham, 2019.

Buber M., *Tales of the Hasidim*, Translated by Olga Marx, Schoken Books, New York, 1948.

Derrida J., *The Gift of Death and Literature in Secret*, Second Edition, Translated by David Wills, University of Chicago Press, Chicago, 2008.

Hirschman O.A., *Exit, Voice and Loyalty. Responses to Decline in Firms*, Organizations, And States, Cambridge, MA, 1972.

Hirschman O.A., *A Propensity to Self-Subversion*, Harvard University Press, Cambridge, MA, 1998.

Jankélévitch V., *Le Pur et l'Impur*, Flammarion, Paris, 1960.

Kierkegaard S., *Fear and Trembling and the Sickness unto Death* (1843), Translated by Walter Lowrie, Princeton University Press, Princeton, 2013.

Loria A., *The Economic Foundations of Society*, Sonnenschein, London, 1904.

Martini C.M., *Per amore, per voi, per sempre. Parole ai consacrati*, Ancora, Milano, 2013.

Merleau-Ponty M., *In Praise of Philosophy and Other Essays* (1953), Translated by John Wilde, James Edie, John O'Neill, Northwestern University Press, Evanston, 1988.

Nussbaum M., *The Fragility of Goodness: Luck and Ethics in Greek Tragedy and Philosophy*, Cambridge University Press, Cambridge, 1986.

Sartre J., *Being and Nothingness*, Translated by Hazel E. Barnes, Washington Square Press, New York, 1992.

Schumpeter J.A., *Capitalism, Socialism and Democracy*, Harper & Brothers, New York, 1942.

Smith A., *The Theory of Moral Sentiments*, Clarendon Press, Oxford, 1759 [1976].

Smith A., *An Inquiry into the Nature and Causes of the Wealth of Nations*, Clarendon Press, Oxford, 1776 [1976].

Weil S., *Gravity and Grace*, Routledge & Kegan Paul, London, 2002 [1952].

West T.G., *Plato's Apology of Socrates. An interpretation, with a new translation*, Cornell University Press, Ithaca, 1979.